THE **TESTING** SERIES
PSYCHOMETRIC
TESTS

THE **TESTING** SERIES
expert advice on interview preparation

how2become

Orders: Please contact How2become Ltd,
Suite 2, 50 Churchill Square Business Centre, Kings Hill, Kent ME19 4YU.

Telephone: (44) 0845 643 1299 - Lines are open Monday to Friday 9am until 5pm.
Fax: (44) 01732 525965.
You can also order via the email address info@how2become.co.uk.

ISBN: 9781907558214

First published 2011

Typeset for How2become Ltd by Good Golly Design, Canada, goodgolly.ca.

Printed in Great Britain for How2become Ltd
by Bell & Bain Ltd, 303 Burnfield Road, Thornliebank, Glasgow G46 7UQ.

CONTENTS

FREE ONLINE PSYCHOMETRIC TESTS

Get instant access to hundred's of online psychometric test questions at the following website:

PSYCHOMETRICTESTSONLINE.CO.UK

WELCOME

Dear Sir/Madam,

Welcome to your new guide, Psychometric Tests. This guide contains hundreds of sample test questions that are appropriate for anyone who is preparing for any type of psychometric test.

An ever increasing number of jobs now require you to sit some form of psychometric test that is based around the key requirements for the role. The more common types of psychometric test include:

- Verbal reasoning

- Numerical reasoning

- Abstract reasoning

- Spatial reasoning

- Mechanical comprehension

The results of the tests are designed to provide the employer with a measure of candidates 'suitability' for a specific post. In the majority of cases, the higher scores you achieve during the test, the more opportunities you will have at your disposal. The key to success is to obviously try your hardest to get 100% correct answers in the test that you are undertaking. If you aim for 100% in your preparation for the tests, then you are far more likely to achieve the job or career that you want. Whilst this advice may appear to be obvious you would be surprised at how many people carry out little or no preparation in the build up to their test.

We have deliberately supplied you with lots of sample questions to assist you. This is the only way that you will improve your performance. It is crucial that when you get a question wrong, you take the time to find out why you got it wrong. Understanding the question is very important.

Finally, even if you are preparing for a test that only requires you to sit one type of psychometric test, numerical reasoning for example, you should still try the questions in the guide that are designed for other areas, such as spatial reasoning, mechanical comprehension and verbal reasoning. Any form of psychometric testing will help you to improve your performance on the day.

Good luck and best wishes,

The how2become team

The How2become team

PREFACE

BY RICHARD MCMUNN

It's probably important that I start off by explaining a little bit about myself, my background, and also why I'm suitably qualified to help you pass your psychometric test.

At the time of writing I am 39 years old and live in the sea-side town of Whitstable which is located on the North Kent coast. I left school at the usual age of 16 and joined the Royal Navy, serving on-board HMS Invincible as part of 800 Naval Air Squadron which formed part of the Fleet Air Arm. There I was at the age of 16, travelling the world and working as an engineer on Sea Harrier jets! It was fantastic and I loved every minute of it. After four years I left the Royal Navy and joined Kent Fire and Rescue Service as a firefighter. Over the next 17 years I worked my way up through the ranks to the position of Assistant Divisional Officer. During my time in the Fire Service I spent a lot of time working as an instructor at the Fire Brigade Training Centre. I was also involved in the selection process for assessing candidates who wanted to join the job. Therefore, my knowledge and experience gained so far in life has been invaluable in helping people like you to pass any type of selection process. I am sure you will find this guide an invaluable resource during your preparation for any type of psychometric test.

I have always been fortunate in the fact that I persevere at everything I do. I've understood that if I keep working hard in life then I will always be successful; or I will achieve whatever it is that I want to achieve. This is an

important lesson that I want you to take on-board straight away. If you work hard and persevere, then success will come your way. The same rule applies whilst preparing for a job selection; if you work hard and try lots of test questions, then you will be successful.

Finally, it is very important that you believe in your own abilities. It does not matter if you have no qualifications. It does not matter if you are currently weak in the area of psychometric testing. What does matter is self-belief, self-discipline and a genuine desire to improve and become successful.

Best wishes,

Richard McMunn

Richard McMunn

TIPS FOR PASSING PSYCHOMETRIC TESTS

There's no two ways about it, the most effective way in which you can prepare for psychometric tests is to carry out lots of sample test questions. When I say lots, I mean lots!

Before I provide you with a host of test questions for many of the different tests you might encounter, here are a few important tips for you to consider:

> It is important that, before you sit your test, you find out the type(s) of test you will be required to undertake. You should also take steps to find out if the tests will be timed and also whether or not they will be 'multiple-choice' based questions. If the tests that you will be required to undertake are timed and of multiple-choice in nature, then I strongly advise that you practice this type of test question.

> Variety is the key to success. Even if you are only required to sit one type of test, for example numerical reasoning, I still recommend that you attempt a variety of different test questions, such as verbal reasoning, fault analysis, spatial reasoning and mechanical reasoning etc. This will undoubtedly improve your overall ability to pass the test that you are required to undertake.

> Confidence is an important part of test preparation. Have you ever sat a timed test and your mind goes blank? This is because your mind is focused on negative thoughts and your belief that you will fail the test. If you practice plenty of test questions under timed conditions then your confidence will grow. If your confidence is at its peak at the commencement of the test then there is no doubt that you will actually look forward to sitting it, as opposed to being fearful of the outcome.

> Whilst this is a very basic tip that may appear obvious, many people neglect to follow it. Make sure that you get a good nights sleep the night before your assessment. Research has shown that those people who have regular 'good' sleep are far more likely to concentrate better during psychometric tests.

> Try practicing numerical test questions in your head, without writing down your workings out. This is very difficult to accomplish, but it is excellent practice for the real test. Also, practice numerical reasoning tests without a calculator. If you are permitted to use a calculator at the test, make sure you know how to use one!

> You are what you eat! In the week prior to the test eat and drink healthily. Avoid cigarettes, alcohol and food with high fat content. The reason for this is that all of these will make you feel sluggish and you will not perform at your peak. On the morning of your assessment eat a healthy breakfast such as porridge and a banana.

> Drink plenty of water, always!

> If you have any special needs that need to be catered for ensure you inform the assessment centre staff prior to the assessment day. I have met people in the past who are fearful of telling the assessment staff that they are dyslexic. You will not be treated negatively; in fact the exact opposite. They will give you extra time in the tests which can only work in your favour.

Now that I have provided you with a number of important tips, take the time to work through the many different sample test questions that are contained within the guide. You will need a stop watch in order to assess your performance against the time constraints for each test.

CHAPTER 1
VERBAL REASONING TESTS

Most employers who use psychometric tests in job selection will include a verbal reasoning or verbal ability test of some form. This is because there are very few graduate careers which don't require the ability to understand, analyse and interpret written information, often of a complex or specialised nature.

On the following pages you will find a number of practice verbal reasoning tests to assist you during your preparation. If, during the real test you find yourself struggling with a question, simply move on to the next one, but remember to leave the answer sheet blank for the particular question that you have not answered. If you then have time at the end, go back to the question(s) you have left and have another go. If you are still unable to answer the question then it is sometimes worth 'guessing' as you still have a '1 in 5' chance of getting it right. However, some assessors will deduct marks for incorrect answers so beware. In the real test you won't have much time to complete the questions so you must work quickly and accurately.

In the questions that follow you will be required to answer the questions as either true, false or cannot say based on the information provided. It is important that you base your answers solely on the information provided within the text.

Take a look at the tests on the following pages. Allow yourself 15 minutes to complete the 15 questions. Write your answer down in the box provided.

VERBAL REASONING TEST 1

Read the following information before answering the questions

Car A is red in colour and has 11 months left on the current MOT. The tax is due in 4 months time. The car has a full service history and has completed 34,000 miles. The car has had 3 owners.

Car B is black in colour and has a full 12 months MOT. The tax is not due for another 12 months. The car has completed 3,445 miles and has only had 1 owner. There is a full service history with the car.

Car C is red in colour and has no tax. The MOT is due to run out in 12 weeks time and the car has no service history. The speedometer reading is 134,000 miles and the car has had a total of 11 owners.

Car D is black in colour and has 11 months left on the current MOT. The tax is due in 6 months time. The car has no service history and has completed 34,000 miles. The car has only had 1 owner.

Car E is red in colour and has 7 months tax. The MOT runs out in 7 months time. The car has a partial service history and has completed 97,000 miles. It has had a total of 4 owners.

Question 1

You want a car that is red in colour and has a full service history with less than 100,000 miles. Which car would you choose?

A. Car A   B. Car B   C. Car C   D. Car D   E. Car E

Answer ☐

Question 2

You want a car that has more than 6 months tax. You are not concerned about the colour but you also want 12 months MOT. Which car would you choose?

A. Car A   B. Car B   C. Car C   D. Car D   E. Car E

Answer ☐

Question 3

You want a car that is red in colour and has had no more than 4 owners. You want a minimum of 6 months tax. The mileage is irrelevant but you do want at least 7 months MOT. Which car would you choose?

A. Car A   B. Car B   C. Car C   D. Car D   E. Car E

Answer

VERBAL REASONING TEST 2

FLIGHT A, outbound, leaves at 8am and arrives at 1pm. The cost of the flight is £69 but this does not include a meal or refreshments. The return flight departs at 3am and arrives at its destination at 8am.

FLIGHT B, outbound, leaves at 3pm and arrives at 8pm. The cost of the flight is £97 and this includes a meal and refreshments. The return flight departs at 1pm and arrives at its destination at 5pm.

FLIGHT C, outbound, leaves at 4pm and arrives at 10pm. The cost of the flight is £70 but this does not include a meal or refreshments. The return flight departs at 10am and arrives at its destination at 4pm.

FLIGHT D, outbound, leaves at midnight and arrives at 3am. The cost of the flight is £105, which does include a meal and refreshments. The return flight departs at 3pm and arrives at 6pm.

FLIGHT E, outbound, leaves at 5am and arrives at 12noon. The cost of the flight is £39, which includes a meal and refreshments. The return flight departs at 5pm and arrives at its destination at midnight.

Question 1

You want a flight where the outbound flight arrives before 2pm on the day of departure. You don't want to pay any more than £50. Which flight would you choose?

A. Flight A   B. Flight B   C. Flight C   D. Flight D   E. Flight E

Answer [   ]

Question 2

You don't want to pay more than £100 for the flight. You want a meal and the outbound departure time must be in the afternoon. Which flight would you choose?

A. Flight A   B. Flight B   C. Flight C   D. Flight D   E. Flight E

Answer [   ]

Question 3

You want a return flight that departs in the afternoon between 12noon and 6pm. The cost of the flight must be below £100 and you do want a meal. The return flight must arrive at your destination before 6pm. Which flight would you choose?

A. Flight A   B. Flight B   C. Flight C   D. Flight D   E. Flight E

Answer

VERBAL REASONING TEST 3

Janet and Steve have been married for 27 years. They have a daughter called Jessica who is 25 years old. They all want to go on holiday together but cannot make up their minds where to go. Janet's first choice would be somewhere hot and sunny abroad. Her second choice would be somewhere in their home country that involves a sporting activity. She does not like hill climbing or walking holidays but her third choice would be a skiing holiday. Steve's first choice would be a walking holiday in the hills somewhere in their home country and his second choice would be a sunny holiday abroad. He does not enjoy skiing. Jessica's first choice would be a skiing holiday and her second choice would be a sunny holiday abroad. Jessica's third choice would be a walking holiday in the hills of their home country.

Question 1

Which holiday are all the family most likely to go on together?

A. Skiing
B. Walking
C. Holiday Abroad
D. Sporting activity holiday
E. Cannot say

Answer

Question 2

If Steve and Jessica were to go on holiday together where would they be most likely to go?

A. Sunny holiday abroad
B. Skiing
C. Cannot say
D. Sporting activity holiday
E. Walking

Answer

Question 3

Which holiday are Janet and Steve most likely to go on together?

A. Cannot say
B. Walking
C. Sporting activity holiday
D. Skiing
E. Sunny holiday abroad

Answer

VERBAL REASONING TEST 4

Barry and Bill work at their local supermarket in the town of Whiteham. Barry works every day except Wednesdays. The supermarket is run by Barry's brother Elliot who is married to Sarah. Sarah and Elliot have 2 children called Marcus and Michelle who are both 7 years old and they live in the road adjacent to the supermarket. Barry lives in a town called Redford, which is 7 miles from Whiteham. Bill's girlfriend Maria works in a factory in her hometown of Brownhaven. The town of Redford is 4 miles from Whiteham and 6 miles from the seaside town of Tenford. Sarah and Elliot take their children on holiday to Tenford twice a year and Barry usually gives them a lift in his car. Barry's mum lives in Tenford and he tries to visit her once a week at 2pm when he is not working.

Question 1

Which town does Elliot live in?

A. Redford   B. Whiteham   C. Brownhaven   D. Tenford   E. Cannot say

Answer [ ]

Question 2

On which day of the week does Barry visit his mother?

A. Cannot say   B. Monday   C. Tuesday   D. Wednesday   E. Thursday

Answer [ ]

Question 3

Bill and Maria live together in Brownhaven.

A. True   B. False   C. Cannot say

Answer [ ]

VERBAL REASONING TEST 5

FLAT A is located in a town. It is 12 miles from the nearest train station. It has 2 bedrooms and is located on the ground floor. The monthly rental is £450 and the council tax is £50 per month. The lease is for 6 months.

FLAT B is located in the city centre and is 2 miles from the nearest train station. It is located on the 3rd floor. The monthly rental is £600 and the council tax is £130 per month. The lease is for 6 months and it has 3 bedrooms.

FLAT C is located in the city centre and is 3 miles from the nearest train station. It is located on the 1st floor and has 1 bedroom. The monthly rental is £550 and the council tax is £100 per month. The lease is for 12 months.

FLAT D is located in a town. The monthly rental is £395 per month and the council tax is £100 per month. It is located on the ground floor and the lease is for 6 months. It is 18 miles from the nearest train station. The flat has 2 bedrooms.

FLAT E is located in a village and is 12 miles from the nearest train station. It has 3 bedrooms and is located on the 2nd floor. The monthly rental is £375 and the council tax is £62.

Question 1

You want a flat that is within 10 miles of the nearest train station and is located on the 1st floor or lower. The combined monthly rent/council tax bill must be no greater than £600. Which flat would you choose?

A. FLAT A
B. FLAT B
C. FLAT C
D. FLAT D
E. NONE OF THE ABOVE.

Answer

Question 2

You want a flat that has at least 2 bedrooms and has a combined monthly rent/council tax bill that does not exceed £450. Which flat would you choose?

A. FLAT A
B. FLAT B
C. FLAT C
D. FLAT D
E. FLAT E

Answer

Question 3

You want a flat that has a combined monthly rent/council tax bill that is not in excess of £600, is within 20 miles of the nearest train station and has a lease of at least 6 months. Which flat would you choose?

A. FLAT A
B. FLAT B
C. FLAT C
D. FLAT D
E. FLAT E

Answer

ANSWERS TO VERBAL REASONING TESTS

VERBAL REASONING TEST 1

1. A

2. B

3. E

VERBAL REASONING TEST 2

1. E

2. B

3. B

VERBAL REASONING TEST 3

1. C

2. A

3. E

VERBAL REASONING TEST 4

1. B

2. D

3. C

VERBAL REASONING TEST 5

1. E

2. E

3. C

VERBAL ABILITY TEST

During this part of the test you will be required to answer 30 questions in 9 minutes, which equates to an average of approximately 18 seconds per question. This test is designed to assess your English language skills. The test is multiple-choice in nature and in the real test you will have 5 options to choose from. The most effective way to prepare for this type of test is to practice sample questions under timed conditions. Other ways of improving your ability include carrying out crosswords, word searches or any other tests that require an ability to work with the English language. You may also decide to purchase your own psychometric test booklet, which can be obtained from all good websites including www.how2become.co.uk.

Take a look at the following sample question.

Sample question 1

Which of the following words is the odd one out?

A. Spanner   B. Pliers   C. Hammer   D. Brush   E. Drill

The answer is D – Brush. This is because all of the other items are tools and the brush is an item used for cleaning, therefore the odd one out.

Now take a look at the next sample question.

Sample question 2

The following sentence has one word missing. Which word makes the best sense of the sentence?

He had been _____ for hours and was starting to lose his concentration.

A. studying   B. sleeping   C. complaining   D. walk   E. targeting

The correct answer is A – studying, as this word makes best sense of the sentence.

Now try verbal ability exercise 1 that follows. There are 30 questions and you have 9 minutes in which to complete them.

VERBAL ABILITY TEST 1

Question 1

Which of the following words is the odd one out?

A. Car   B. Aeroplane   C. Train   D. Bicycle   E. House

Answer ☐

Question 2

Which of the following is the odd one out?

A. Right   B. White   C. Dart   D. Bright   E. Sight

Answer ☐

Question 3

The following sentence has one word missing. Which word makes the best sense of the sentence?

The mechanic worked on the car for 3 hours. At the end of the 3 hours he was.....

A. Home   B. Rich   C. Crying   D. Exhausted   E. Thinking

Answer ☐

Question 4

The following sentence has 2 words missing. Which two words make best sense of the sentence?

The man _____ to walk along the beach with his dog. He threw the stick and the dog _____ it.

A. hated/chose
B. decided/wanted
C. liked/chased
D. hurried/chased
E. hated/loved

Answer ☐

Question 5

In the line below, the word outside of the brackets will only go with three of the words inside the brackets to make longer words. Which ONE word will it NOT go with?

A	B	C	D
In (direct	famous	desirable	cart)

Answer [ ]

Question 6

In the line below, the word outside of the brackets will only go with three of the words inside the brackets to make longer words. Which ONE word will it NOT go with?

A	B	C	D
In (decisive	reference	destructible	convenience)

Answer [ ]

Question 7

In the line below, the word outside of the brackets will only go with three of the words inside the brackets to make longer words. Which ONE word will it NOT go with?

A	B	C	D
A (float	bout	part	peck)

Answer [ ]

Question 8

Which of the following words is the odd one out?

A. Pink   B. Salt   C. Ball   D. Red   E. Grey

Answer [ ]

Question 9
Which of the following words is the odd one out?

A. Run   B. Jog   C. Walk   D. Sit   E. Sprint

Answer [　　]

Question 10
Which of the following words is the odd one out?

A. Eagle   B. Plane   C. Squirrel   D. Cloud   E. Bird

Answer [　　]

Question 11
Which of the following words is the odd one out?

A. Gold   B. Ivory   C. Platinum   D. Bronze   E. Silver

Answer [　　]

Question 12
Which of the following is the odd one out?

A. Pond   B. River   C. Stream   D. Brook   E. Ocean

Answer [　　]

Question 13
Which of the following is the odd one out?

A. Wood   B. Chair   C. Table   D. Cupboard   E. Stool

Answer [　　]

Question 14

Which three letter word can be placed in front of the following words to make a new word?

Time   Break   Light   Dreamer

Answer [   ]

Question 15

Which four letter word can be placed in front of the following words to make a new word?

Box   Bag   Age   Card

Answer [   ]

Question 16

The following sentence has one word missing. Which ONE word makes the best sense of the sentence?

After walking for an hour in search of the pub, David decided it was time to turn _____ and go back home.

A. up   B. in   C. home   D. around   E. through

Answer [   ]

Question 17

The following sentence has one word missing. Which ONE word makes the best sense of the sentence?

We are continually updating the site and would be _____ to hear any comments you may have.

A. Pleased   B. Worried   C. Available   D. Suited   E. Scared

Answer [   ]

Question 18

The following sentence has two words missing. Which TWO words make the best sense of the sentence?

The Fleet Air Arm is the Royal Navy's air force. It numbers some 6,200 people, _____ is 11.5% of the _____ Royal Naval strength.

A. which/total
B. and/total
C. which/predicted
D. and/corporate
E. which/approximately

Answer

Question 19

The following sentence has one word missing. Which ONE word makes the best sense of the sentence?

The Navy has had to _____ and progress to be ever prepared to defend the British waters from rival forces.

A. develop   B. manoeuvre   C. change   D. seek   E. watch

Answer

Question 20

Which of the following is the odd one out?

A. Cat   B. Dog   C. Hamster   D. Owl   E. Rabbit

Answer

Question 21

Which word best fits the following sentence?

My doctor says I _____ smoke. It's bad for my health.

A. will   B. wouldn't   C. shouldn't   D. like   E. might

Answer

Question 22

Which word best fits the following sentence?

The best thing for a hangover is to go to bed and sleep it   .

A. through   B. over   C. away   D. in   E. off

Answer

Question 23

Complete the following sentence:

By the time Jane arrived at the disco, Andrew _____ .

A. hadn't gone
B. already left
C. has already Left
D. had stayed
E. had already left

Answer

Question 24

Which of the following words is the odd one out?

A. Lawnmower   B. Hose   C. Rake   D. Carpet   E. Shovel

Answer

Question 25

Complete the following sentence:

Karla was offered the job _____ having poor qualifications.

A. although   B. even though   C. with   D. without   E. despite

Answer

Question 26

Complete the following sentence:

Not only _____ to Glasgow but he also visited many other places in Scotland too.

A. did she   B. did he   C. did he go   D. she went   E. she saw

Answer

Question 27

Complete the following sentence:

Now please remember, you _____ the test until the teacher tells you to.

A. shouldn't
B. will not be starting
C. are not to
D. can't
E. are not to start

Answer

Question 28

Which of the following is the odd one out?

A. Strawberry   B. Raspberry   C. Peach   D. Blackberry   E. Blueberry

Answer

Question 29

Which of the following is the odd one out?

A. Football   B. Wrestling   C. Table tennis   D. Golf   E. Rugby

Answer

Question 30

Which of the following is the odd one out?

A. Man   B. Milkman   C. Secretary   D. Police Officer   E. Firefighter

Answer

Now that you have completed verbal ability exercise 1, check your answers carefully before moving on to exercise 2.

ANSWERS TO VERBAL ABILITY TEST 1

1. E	**16.** D
2. C	**17.** A
3. D	**18.** A
4. C	**19.** A
5. D	**20.** D
6. B	**21.** C
7. D	**22.** E
8. D	**23.** E
9. D	**24.** D
10. C	**25.** E
11. B	**26.** C
12. A	**27.** E
13. A	**28.** C
14. Day	**29.** B
15. Post	**30.** A

Once you are satisfied with your answers, move onto verbal ability test 2. You have 9 minutes to complete the 30 questions.

VERBAL ABILITY TEST 2

Question 1
Which one of the following words relates to the other four?

A. Barbeque   B. Stove   C. Sausages   D. Burge   E. Cooking

Answer [ ]

Question 2
Which one of the following words relates to the other four?

A. Television   B. Acting   C. Entertainment   D. Gig   E. Theatre

Answer [ ]

Question 3
Which one of the following words relates to the other four?

A. Running   B. Fitness   C. Swimming   D. Cycling   E. Rowing

Answer [ ]

Question 4
Which one word inside the brackets will not go with the word outside of the bracket?

Ant (acid   agonise   eater   implode   hem)

Answer [ ]

Question 5
Which one word inside the brackets will not go with the word outside of the bracket?

Tin (stone   well   man   smith   foil)

Answer [ ]

Question 6

Which one word inside the brackets will not go with the word outside of the bracket?

Band (mess   width   wagon   leader   master)

Answer ☐

Question 7

Which one word inside the brackets will not go with the word outside of the bracket?

Grip (ping   pier   sack   man   wool)

Answer ☐

Question 8

Which one word inside the brackets will not go with the word outside of the bracket?

Day (dream   light   time   room   ball)

Answer ☐

Question 9

Which of the following sentences has a different meaning to the other four?

A. Richard ended up buying the car for £900.
B. The car was bought by Richard for £900.
C. £900 was the amount Richard spent on the car.
D. The car cost Richard £900.
E. Richard sold the car for £900.

Answer ☐

Question 10

Which of the following sentences has a different meaning to the other four?

A. Sally spent £350 during her shopping trip.
B. During a shopping trip Sally spent £350.
C. Sally made £350 from her shopping trip.
D. The shopping trip cost Sally £350.
E. A total of £350 was spent during Sally's shopping trip.

Answer ☐

Question 11

Which of the following sentences has a different meaning to the other four?

A. Barry lost two stone in weight over a period of 4 months.
B. Over a 4 month period Barry gained two stone in weight.
C. Barry put on two stone in 4 months.
D. Over a period of 4 months Barry put on two stone in weight.
E. Two stone was gained in weight by Barry over a 4 month period.

Answer ☐

Question 12

Which one of the following words relates to the other four?

A. Cardigan   B. Clothes   C. Trousers   D. Shirt   E. Underwear

Answer ☐

Question 13

Which one of the following words relates to the other four?

A. Pear   B. Apple   C. Banana   D. Pineapple   E. Fruit

Answer ☐

Question 14
Which one of the following words relates to the other four?

A. Communicate   B. E mail   C. Telephone   D. Speak   E. Letter

Answer

Question 15
Which one of the following words relates to the other four?

A. Run   B. Cycle   C. Walk   D. Movement   E. Drive

Answer

Question 16
Which of the following sentences has a different meaning to the other four?

A. The bouncer pushed the man to the floor.
B. The man was pushed to the floor by the bouncer.
C. The bouncer was pushed by the man and he fell to the floor.
D. The bouncer pushed the man and he fell to the floor.
E. The man was pushed by the bouncer to the floor.

Answer

Question 17
Which one word inside the brackets will not go with the word outside of the bracket?

Run (around   back   charm   lets   off)

Answer

Question 18
Which one word inside the brackets will not go with the word outside of the bracket?

Pot (hole   stir   belly   ability   able)

Answer

Question 19

Which of the following is the odd one out?

A. Apples   B. Parsnips   C. Peas   D. Sprouts   E. Carrots

Answer ☐

Question 20

Which of the following is the odd one out?

A. Circle   B. Rectangle   C. Flat   D. Square   E. Sphere

Answer ☐

Question 21

The following sentence has one word missing. Which word makes the best sense of the sentence?

Sid _____ that he wanted to go home earlier than he originally anticipated.

A. told   B. thought   C. boasted   D. decided   E. suddenly

Answer ☐

Question 22

The following sentence has one word missing. Which word makes the best sense of the sentence?

Tony was often seen walking in the park with _____ dog.

A. one   B. slow   C. his   D. ours   E. them

Answer ☐

Question 23

The following sentence has two words missing. Which two words make the best sense of the sentence?

The album _____ at number one in countries such as the United Kingdom and Canada, and _____ the charts in the United States.

A. peaked / topped
B. reached / topped
C. got / then
D. reached / stormed
E. topped / stormed.

Answer

Question 24

The following sentence has two words missing. Which two word makes the best sense of the sentence?

After four hours of looking, the _____ for the _____ puppy was called off.

A. party / search
B. search / missing
C. dog / missing
D. crying / lovely
E. puppy / lovely.

Answer

Question 25

Which of the following sentences has a different meaning to the other four?

A. He drove 80 miles to see his fiancée.
B. The man drove 80 miles so that he could see his fiancée.
C. In order to see his fiancée the man drove 80 miles.
D. After driving 80 miles the man was at last with his fiancée.
E. His fiancée had driven 80 miles to see him.

Answer

Question 26

Which of the following sentences has a different meaning to the other four?

A. It took the man five hours to complete the marathon.
B. The man completed the marathon in five hours.
C. The marathon was completed by the man in five hours.
D. Five hours later the man had completed the marathon.
E. The woman would run the marathon in five hours.

Answer

Question 27

Which one word inside the brackets will not go with the word outside of the bracket?

Run (away   day   down   over   out)

Answer

Question 28

Which one word inside the brackets will not go with the word outside of the bracket?

Can (run   teen   did   non   descent)

Answer

Question 29

The following sentence has two words missing. Which two words make the best sense of the sentence?

The boy accidentally _____ his ball _____ next doors garden.

A. accidentally / into
B. accidentally / through
C. kicked / into
D. aimed / top
E. kicked / accidentally.

Answer

Question 30

The following sentence has two words missing. Which two words make the best sense of the sentence?

It didn't _____ the man long before he was _____ about the food at the restaurant again.

A. take / complaining
B. need / asking
C. take / complimenting
D. take / eating
E. need / complaining.

Answer ☐

Now that you have completed verbal ability exercise 2, take the time to work through your answers carefully before moving onto the next test.

ANSWERS TO VERBAL ABILITY TEST 2

1.	E	**16.**	C
2.	C	**17.**	Charm
3.	B	**18.**	Stir
4.	Implode	**19.**	A
5.	Well	**20.**	E
6.	Mess	**21.**	D
7.	Wool	**22.**	C
8.	Bal	**23.**	A
9.	E	**24.**	B
10.	C	**25.**	E
11.	A	**26.**	E
12.	B	**27.**	Day
13.	E	**28.**	Run
14.	A	**29.**	C
15.	D	**30.**	A

CHAPTER 2
NUMERICAL REASONING TESTS

This type of test is used to determine how accurately you can carry out numerical addition, subtraction, division, multiplication and also interpret numerical information such as charts, graphs and tables. The test will also assess your ability to use fractions, decimals and different formulae. As you can imagine, the most effective way to prepare for this type of test is to carry out lots of sample numerical reasoning test questions, without the aid of a calculator.

During the actual numerical reasoning test that you will be required to sit you will have a specific amount of time to answer each question. It is important that you do not spend too much time on one particular question. Remember that the clock is ticking. Have a go at the first numerical reasoning exercise that follows and use a blank sheet of paper to work out your calculations. Remember to check your answers very carefully. It is important that you check any incorrect answers to see why you got them wrong.

You have 10 minutes in which to answer the 20 questions. Calculators are not permitted.

NUMERICAL REASONING TEST 1

Question 1

Calculate 5.99 + 16.02

A. 19.01   B. 20.01   C. 21.99   D. 22.99   E. 22.01

Answer

Question 2

Calculate 3.47 – 1.20

A. 22.7   B. 2.27   C. 1.27   D. 2.67   E. 0.27

Answer

Question 3

Calculate 98.26 – 62.89

A. 37.35   B. 35.37   C. 36.35   D. 36.37   E. 37.73

Answer

Question 4

Calculate 45.71 – 29.87

A. 14.84   B. 18.88   C. 14.89   D. 15.84   E. 15.85

Answer

Question 5

Calculate 564.87 + 321.60

A. 886.45   B. 886.74   C. 886.47   D. 868.47   E. 868.74

Answer

Question 6
Calculate 16.0 – 9.9

A. 6.9   B. 6.1   C. 7.1   D. 7.9   E. 5.1

Answer [   ]

Question 7
Calculate 1109.12 + 0.8

A. 1109.20   B. 1109.92   C. 1109.02   D. 1110.20   E. 1110.92

Answer [   ]

Question 8
Calculate 4.1 x 3.0

A.	B.	C.	D.	E.
123	9.1	12.41	7.1	12.3

Answer [   ]

Question 9
Calculate 16.8 x 4

A.	B.	C.	D.	E.
67.2	64.8	64.47.1	67.4	67.8

Answer [   ]

Question 10
Calculate 2.2 x 2.2

A.	B.	C.	D.	E.
4.4	44.4	2.84	4.84	8.44

Answer [   ]

Question 11
In the following question what is the value of t?

$$\frac{5\,(t - 32)}{2} = 5$$

A. 64   B. 128   C. 43   D. 34   E. 39

Answer

Question 12
In the following question what is the value of t?

$$\frac{3\,(t + 35)}{6} = 35$$

A. 35   B. 70   C. 75   D. 77   E. 30

Answer

Question 13
In the following question what is the value of t?

$$\frac{9\,(t \times 16)}{5} = 144$$

A. 6   B. 3   C. 9   D. 15   E. 5

Answer

Question 14
In the following question what is the value of t?

$$\frac{4t - 16}{32} = 2$$

A. 5   B. 10   C. 15   D. 20   E. 25

Answer

Question 15

Convert 0.7 to a fraction.

A. 7/10 B. 3/4 C. $7\frac{5}{1}$ D. 1/10 E. 2/3

Answer

Question 16

Convert 2.5 to a fraction.

A. 25/1 B. 3/6 C. $2\frac{1}{2}$ D. 1/25 E. $2\frac{2}{1}$

Answer

Question 17

Convert 3.75 to a fraction.

A. 75/1 B. 1/375 C. $3\frac{1}{75}$ D. 75/3 E. $3\frac{3}{4}$

Answer

Question 18

Convert 3/10 to a decimal.

A. 3.0 B. 0.3 C. 3.33 D. 0.03 E. 0.003

Answer

Question 19

Convert 1/4 to a decimal.

A. 0.025 B. 2.5 C. 0.25 D. 0.4 E. 4.0

Answer

Question 20

Convert 4/5 to a decimal.

A. 0.08 B. 8.0 C. 4.5 D. 5.4 E. 0.8

Answer

ANSWERS TO NUMERICAL REASONING TEST 1

1. E		**11.** D	
2. B		**12.** A	
3. B		**13.** E	
4. D		**14.** D	
5. C		**15.** A	
6. B		**16.** C	
7. B		**17.** E	
8. E		**18.** B	
9. A		**19.** C	
10. D		**20.** E	

Once you are satisfied with your answers move on to numerical test 2. You have 7 minutes to complete the 15 questions. Calculators are not permitted.

NUMERICAL REASONING TEST 2

Look at Table 1 below and then answer the questions that follow.

TABLE 1. The following table lists the type of bonus each member of staff will receive if they reach a specific number of sales per hour they work. The table has not yet been completed. Staff work seven hour shifts. In order to answer the questions you will need to complete the table.

TIME	10 SALES	20 SALES	30 SALES	40 SALES
1st hour	£21.00	£41.50	£60.50	£72.00
2nd hour	£18.00	£35.00	£52.00	£60.00
3rd hour	£15.00	£28.50	£43.50	£50.00
4th hour	–	£22.00	£35.00	£42.00
5th hour	£9.00	–	£26.50	£36.00
6th hour	£6.00	£9.00	–	£32.00
7th hour	£3.00	£3.50	£9.50	–

Note: If a worker achieves 160 sales or more during their 7 hour shift they will receive an additional £50 bonus.

Question 1

If the table was complete how much could a worker earn in bonuses if they reached 10 sales every hour of their 7 hour shift?

A. £81   B. £84   C. £91   D. £85   E. £94

Answer

Question 2

How much would a worker earn in bonuses if they reached 30 sales per hour for the first 3 hours of their shift and 40 sales per hour for the remaining 4 hours of their shift?

A. £292   B. £293   C. £436   D. £246   E. £346

Answer

Question 3

How much would a worker earn in bonuses if they reached 10 sales during their first and last hour, 20 sales during the 2nd and 6th hours, 30 sales during the 3rd and 5th hours and 40 sales during the 4th hour?

A. £230   B. £250   C. £180   D. £181   E. £182

Answer

Look at the following bar chart below before answering the questions that follow.

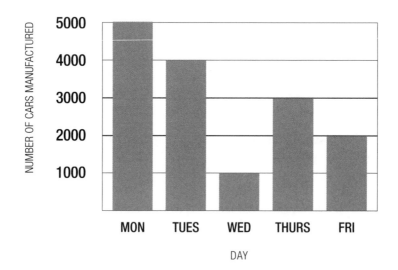

The above chart indicates the total number of cars manufactured per day of the week at the Arlingford Car Depot. Study the graph and answer the questions on the following page.

Question 4

On which day was the number of cars manufactured 80% less than the number manufactured on Monday?

A. Tuesday   B. Wednesday   C. Thursday   D. Friday   E. None

Answer

Question 5

How many cars were produced in total on Tuesday, Wednesday and Friday?

A. 4,000   B. 5,000   C. 6,000   D. 7,000   E. 8,000

Answer

Question 6

What was the average number of cars manufactured per day for the working week?

A. 2,142   B. 2,500   C. 3,000   D. 2,141   E. 2,140

Answer

The following graph indicates the total monthly profits of four competing companies. Study the graph and answer the questions that follow.

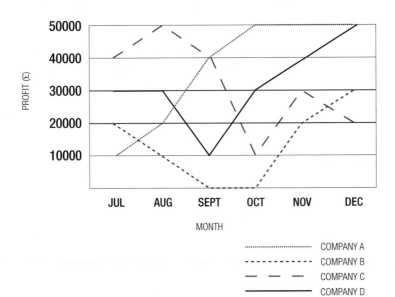

Question 7

Over the 6 month period, which company made the greatest profit?

A. Company A   B. Company B   C. Company C   D. Company D

Answer

Question 8

What is the difference in profits over the 6 month period between company C and company D?

A. £1,000   B. Nothing   C. £2,000   D. £3,000   E. £4,000

Answer

Question 9

What was the total combined 6 month profit for all four companies?

A. £660,000   B. £610,000   C. £630,000   D. £650,000   E. £680,000

Answer

The following table shows the distribution list for a UK based company including the location of delivery, type of package ordered, the quantity ordered and the cost excluding delivery. Study the table before answering the questions that follow.

DATE	LOCATION OF SALES	PACKAGE ORDERED	QUANTITY ORDERED	COST (EXCLUDING DELIVERY)
13th Jan	Kent	Package 1	2	£45
17th Jan	Preston	Package 4	13	£1,600
2nd Feb	Manchester	Package 2	6	£246
3rd Feb	Glasgow	–	12	£270
17th Feb	Fareham	Package 2	8	–
19th Mar	Hudderfield	Package 5	1	£213
20th Mar	Crewe	–	3	£639

Question 10

Which package will be delivered on the 3rd of February?

A. Package 1   B. Package 2   C. Package 4   D. Package 5

Answer

Question 11

What will be the cost (excluding delivery) on the 17th of February?

A. £322   B. £324   C. £326   D. £328   E. £330

Answer

Question 12

Which package is scheduled to be delivered to Crewe on the 20th of March?

A. Package 1   B. Package 2   C. Package 4   D. Package 5

Answer

The following bar chart indicates the total number of people employed by a large international distribution company. Study the chart before answering the questions that follow.

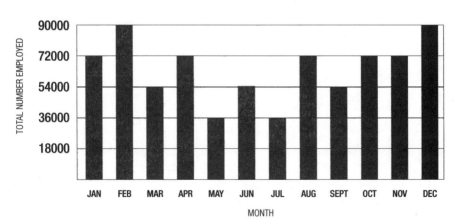

Question 13

What was the average monthly employment figure for the 12 month period?

A. 60,000   B. 50,000   C. 54,500   D. 64,500   E. 74,500

Answer

Question 14

What was the total number of people employed during the second quarter of the year?

A. 62,000   B. 52,000   C. 162,000   D. 152,000   E. 143,000

Answer

Question 15

What was the difference between the number of people employed in the first quarter and the last quarter of the year?

A. 18,000   B. 17,000   C. 16,000   D.   180,000   E. 170,000

Answer

ANSWERS TO NUMERICAL REASONING TEST 2

1. B	**9.** E
2. E	**10.** A
3. A	**11.** D
4. B	**12.** D
5. D	**13.** D
6. C	**14.** C
7. A	**15.** A
8. B	

Once you are satisfied with your answers move on to numerical test 3. You have 15 minutes to complete the 30 questions. Calculators are not permitted

NUMERICAL REASONING TEST 3

Q1. 58 + ? = 87

A. 26   B. 27   C. 28   D. 29   E. 30

Answer ☐

Q2. 101 - ? = 47

A. 51   B. 52   C. 53   D. 54   E. 55

Answer ☐

Q3. ? + 567 = 621

A. 51   B. 52   C. 53   D. 54   E. 65

Answer ☐

Q4. 36 x ? = 252

A. 9   B. 8   C. 7   D. 6   E. 5

Answer ☐

Q5. 8 + 9 + 9 = 13 x ?

A. 4   B. 3   C. 2   D. 1   E. 5

Answer ☐

Q6. (46 + 28) − 4 = ? + 45

A. 36   B. 26   C. 15   D.35   E. 25

Answer ☐

Q7. 84 ÷ ? = 12 + 9

A. 2   B. 4   C. 6   D. 8   E. 3

Answer ☐

Q8. 198 - ? = 58 x 3

A. 23   B. 48   C. 42   D. 46   E. 24

Answer ☐

Q9. 100 ÷ 5 = 99 - ?

A. 19   B. 79   C. 89   D. 69   E. 29

Answer ☐

Q10. 41 x 8 = 1312 ÷ ?

A. 3   B. 4   C. 5   D. 6   E. None of these

Answer ☐

Q11. Following the pattern shown in the number sequence below, what is the missing number?

6   18   54   ?   486   1458

A. 97   B. 302   C. 249   D. 162   E. 163

Answer ☐

Q12. If you count from 1 to 100, how many number 5s will you pass on the way?

A. 10   B. 19   C. 11   D. 20   E. 21

Answer ☐

Q13. 50% of 842 = ?

A. 241   B. 240   C. 420   D. 402   E. 421

Answer ☐

Q14. 75% of 3300 = ?

A. 2745   B. 2475   C. 2455   D. 3000   E. 2905

Answer [　]

Q15. 80% of 800 = ?

A. 860   B. 880   C. 640   D. 600   E. 680

Answer [　]

Q16. 15% of 200 = ?

A. 45   B. 35   C. 30   D. 15   E. 7.5

Answer [　]

Q17. 45% of 500 = ?

A. 200   B. 225   C. 240   D. 245   E. 725

Answer [　]

Q18. 7% of 350 = ?

A. 24.5   B. 20.5   C. 245   D. 205   E. 25.5

Answer [　]

Q19. 9952 – 2599 = ?

A. 7535   B. 3577   C. 5733   D. 3753   E. 7353

Answer [　]

Q20. 9 x 4.5 = ?

A. 40   B. 39.5   C. 41.5   D. 40.5   E. 42

Answer [　]

Q21. 1888 ÷ 4 = ?

A. 422   B. 472   C. 247   D. 427   E. 224

Answer

Q22. 8665 − 856 = ?

A. 8097 B. 7808   C. 7809 D. 8079 E. 7089

Answer

Q23. 663 + 113 = ?

A. 76   B. 74   C. 775   D. 716   E. 776

Answer

Q24. A rectangle has an area of 48cm². The length of one side is 6cm. What is the perimeter of the rectangle?

A. 24 inches B. 24cm C. 18cm D. 28cm E. 28 inches

Answer

Q25. A square has a perimeter of 36cm. What is the length of one side?

A. 81cm B. 72cm C. 18cm D. 81 metres E. 9cm

Answer

Q26. During the Air Traffic Controller Test a candidate achieves 60%. If the maximum possible score was 80, what score did the candidate achieve?

A. 60   B. 40   C. 44   D. 48   E. 50

Answer

Q27. Is 1589 divisible by 7?

A. Yes   B. No

Answer

Q28. During the Air Traffic Controller Test a candidate achieves 40%. If the maximum possible score was 85, what score did the candidate achieve?

A. 34   B. 35   C. 36   D. 44   E. 45

Answer

Q29. One side of a rectangle is 15cm. If the area of the rectangle is 255cm², what is the length of the other side?

A. 15cm   B. 17cm   C. 6cm   D. 7cm   E. 9cm

Answer

Q30. A rectangle has an area of 144cm². The length of one side is 16cm. What is the perimeter?

A. 8cm   B. 16cm   C. 10cm   D. 12cm   E. None of these.

Answer

ANSWERS TO NUMERICAL REASONING TEST 3

1.	D	**16.**	C
2.	D	**17.**	B
3.	D	**18.**	A
4.	C	**19.**	E
5.	C	**20.**	D
6.	E	**21.**	B
7.	B	**22.**	C
8.	E	**23.**	E
9.	B	**24.**	D
10.	B	**25.**	E
11.	D	**26.**	D
12.	D	**27.**	A
13.	E	**28.**	A
14.	B	**29.**	B
15.	C	**30.**	E

Once you are satisfied with your answers move on to numerical test 4.
You have 15 minutes to complete the 30 questions. Calculators are
not permitted.

NUMERICAL REASONING TEST 4

During numerical reasoning test 4 you have 15 minutes in which to answer
the 30 questions. Calculators are not permitted.

Q1. Calculate 6.99 + 18.09

    A. 25.08
    B. 24.08
    C. 24.80
    D. 25.80
    E. 23.08

Answer

Q2. Calculate 13.26 − 2.22

    A. 11.4
    B. 11.04
    C. 10.04
    D. 12.04
    E. 11.06

Answer

Q3. Calculate 138.22 − 12.45

    A. 126.77
    B. 127.77
    C. 152.77
    D. 127.55
    E. 125.77

Answer

Q4. Calculate 4671.80 − 27.88

    A. 4643.92
    B. 4346.29
    C. 4634.92
    D. 4432.92
    E. 4634.02

Answer

Q5. Calculate 278.09 + 325.80

    A. 603.99
    B. 630.89
    C. 603.89
    D. 503.89
    E. 599.09

    Answer

Q6. Calculate 17.1 – 9.8

    A. 8.3
    B. 6.3
    C. 7.2
    D. 7.6
    E. 7.3

    Answer

Q7. Calculate 5.6 x 2.2

    A. 10.12
    B. 10.62
    C. 11.32
    D. 12.32
    E. 13.22

    Answer

Q8. Calculate 5.1 x 4.7

    A. 23.79
    B. 23.97
    C. 24.97
    D. 20.7
    E. 20.8

    Answer

Q9. Calculate 19.8 x 3

    A. 27.24
    B. 59.4
    C. 58.9
    D. 57.4
    E. 57.24

Answer

Q10. Calculate 4.4 x 4.4

    A. 88.88
    B. 44.44
    C. 16.16
    D. 19.36
    E. 8.44

Answer

Q11. Convert 0.75 to a fraction?

    A. 1/75
    B. 3/4
    C. 7/5
    D. 2/5
    E. 4/6

Answer

Q12. Jake wants to lose 10 kilograms. After 3 months he has lost ¾ of this amount. How much has lost?

    A. 5 kg
    B. 4 kg
    C. 7 kg
    D. 7.5 kg
    E. 8 kg

Answer

Q13. Hayley weighs 75 kilograms. If she wants to lose 8% of her total body weight, how much does she need to lose?

    A. 6kg
    B. 7kg
    C. 8kg
    D. 60kg
    E. 70kg

Answer

Q14. If r = 45 and s = 965, then s − r =

    A. 290
    B. 92
    C. 920
    D. 930
    E. 935

Answer

Q15. 15 out of 75 hospital patients have leg injuries. What percentage of patients do not have leg injuries?

    A. 60
    B. 20
    C. 11.25
    D. 12
    E. 80

Answer

Q16. Alison has been keeping a record of how much she has been withdrawing from the cash point machine. Over the last 10 weeks she has withdrawn the following amounts:

£10 £20 £80 £60 £20 £10 £90 £100 £50 £30

What percentage of her withdrawals are under £60?

A. 40%

B. 50%

C. 60%

D. 70%

E. 65%

Answer

Q17. 1/5 x 2/5 = ?

A. 2/5

B. 2/25

C. 3/25

D. 4/25

E. 2/525

Answer

Q18. 1/3 x 1/3 = ?

A. 1/9

B. 1/33

C. 1/3

D. 1/39

E. 3/4

Answer

Q19. ½ ÷ ¾ = ?

A. 2/3

B. 4/5

C. ¾

D. 7/8

E. 3/5

Answer

Q20. What is the number 55.87244 correct to three decimal places?

    A. 55.873

    B. 55.87

    C. 55.882

    D. 55.872

    E. 55.883

Answer ☐

Q21. The clock above reads 10:10 am. How many degrees will the large (minute) hand have turned when the time reaches 11:00 am?

    A. 180°

    B. 250°

    C. 270°

    D. 300°

    E. 320°

Answer ☐

Q22. The clock above reads 10:10 am. How many degrees will the large (minute) hand have turned when the time reaches 11:30 am?

    A. 360°

    B. 380°

    C. 400°

    D. 460°

    E. 480°

Answer ☐

Q23. The clock above reads 10:10 am. How many degrees will the large (minute) hand have turned when the time reaches 11:07 am?

A. 342°
B. 340°
C. 322°
D. 312°
E. 307°

Answer

Q24. The clock above reads 10:10 am. How many degrees will the small (hour) hand have turned when the time reaches 8:10 pm?

A. 60°
B. 300°
C. 360°
D. 180°
E. 270°

Answer

Q25. The clock above reads 10:10 am. How many degrees will the small (hour) hand have turned when the time reaches 11:10 pm?

A. 305°
B. 390°
C. 360°
D. 180°
E. 270°

Answer

Q26. The clock above reads 10:10 am. How many degrees will the small (hour) hand have turned when the time reaches 13:10 pm?

    A. 45°
    B. 30°
    C. 15°
    D. 180°
    E. 90°

Answer

Q27. The Fire Service reports the following number and type of fires in a 12 month period:

Car fires	100
Chimney fires	200
House fires	50
Derelict building fires	350
Rubbish fires	300

What percentage of fires were chimney fires?

    A. 10%
    B. 15%
    C. 20%
    D. 25%
    E. 30%

Answer

Q28. The Fire Service reports the following number and type of fires in a 12 month period:

Car fires	200
Chimney fires	100
House fires	350
Derelict building fires	150
Rubbish fires	200

What percentage of fires were derelict building fires?

A. 10%
B. 15%
C. 20%
D. 25%
E. 30%

Answer

Q29. 1200 x 0.4 = ?

A. 560
B. 440
C. 990
D. 330
E. 480

Answer

Q30. 760 x 0.2 = ?

A. 125
B. 122
C. 152
D. 142
E. 150

Answer

ANSWERS TO NUMERICAL REASONING TEST 4

1.	A	**16.**	C
2.	B	**17.**	B
3.	E	**18.**	A
4.	A	**19.**	A
5.	C	**20.**	D
6.	E	**21.**	D
7.	D	**22.**	E
8.	B	**23.**	A
9.	B	**24.**	B
10.	D	**25.**	B
11.	B	**26.**	E
12.	D	**27.**	C
13.	A	**28.**	B
14.	C	**29.**	E
15.	E	**30.**	C

Once you are satisfied with your answers, move on to numerical test 5.
You have 15 minutes to complete the 30 questions.

NUMERICAL REASONING TEST 5

Question 1

37 + ? = 95

A. 85   B. 45   C. 58   D. 57   E. 122

Answer

Question 2

86 - ? = 32

A. 54   B. 45   C. 108   D. 118   E. 68

Answer

Question 3

? + 104 = 210

A. 601   B. 314   C. 61   D.106   E.110

Answer

Question 4

109 x ? = 218

A. 1   B. 109   C. 12   D. 10   E. 2

Answer

Question 5

6 + 9 + 15 = 15 x ?

A. 15   B. 2   C. 3   D. 4   E. 5

Answer

Question 6

(34 + 13) − 4 = ? + 3

A. 7   B. 47   C. 51   D. 40   E. 37

Answer ☐

Question 7

35 ÷ ? = 10 + 7.5

A. 2   B. 10   C. 4   D. 1   E. 17

Answer ☐

Question 8

7 x ? = 28 x 3

A. 2   B. 3   C. 21   D. 15   E. 12

Answer ☐

Question 9

100 ÷ 4 = 67 - ?

A. 42   B. 24   C. 57   D. 333   E. 2

Answer ☐

Question 10

32 x 9 = 864 ÷ ?

A. 288   B. 3   C. 882   D. 4   E. None of these

Answer ☐

Question 11

Following the pattern shown in the number sequence below, what is the missing number?

3 9 18 ? 72 144

A. 27   B. 36   C. 49   D. 21   E. 63

Answer ☐

Question 12

If you count from 1 to 100, how many 6s will you pass on the way?

A. 10   B. 19   C. 20   D. 11   E. 21

Answer ☐

Question 13

50% of 350 = ?

A. 170   B. 25   C. 175   D. 170   E. 700

Answer ☐

Question 14

75% of 1000 = ?

A.   75   B. 0.75   C. 75000   D. 750   E. 7.5

Answer ☐

Question 15

40% of 40 = ?

A. 160   B. 4   C. 1600   D. 1.6   E. 16

Answer ☐

Question 16

25% of 75 = ?

A. 18   B. 18.75   C. 18.25   D. 25   E. 17.25

Answer ☐

Question 17

15% of 500 = ?

A. 75   B. 50   C. 0.75   D. 0.505   E. 750

Answer ☐

Question 18

5% of 85 = ?

A. 4   B. 80   C. 4.25   D. 0.85   E. 89.25

Answer ☐

Question 19

9876 – 6789 = ?

A. 3078   B. 3085   C. 783   D. 3086   E. 3087

Answer ☐

Question 20

27 x 4 = ?

A. 106   B. 107   C. 108   D. 109   E. 110

Answer ☐

Question 21

96 ÷ 4 = ?

A. 22   B. 23   C. 24   D. 25   E. 26

Answer [ ]

Question 22

8765 – 876 = ?

A. 9887   B. 7888   C. 7890   D. 7998   E. 7889

Answer [ ]

Question 23

623 + 222 = ?

A. 840   B. 845   C. 740   D. 745   E. 940

Answer [ ]

Question 24

A rectangle has an area of 24cm². The length of one side is 8cm. What is the perimeter of the rectangle?

A. 22 inches   B. 24cm   C. 18cm   D. 22cm   E. 18 inches

Answer [ ]

Question 25

A square has a perimeter of 36cm. Its area is 81cm². What is the length of one side?

A. 9cm   B. 18cm   C. 9 metres   D. 18 metres   E. 16cm

Answer [ ]

Question 26

Which of the following is the same as 25/1000?

A. 0.25   B. 0.025   C. 0.0025   D. 40   E. 25000

Answer ☐

Question 27

Is 33 divisible by 3?

A. Yes   B. No

Answer ☐

Question 28

What is 49% of 1100?

A. 535   B. 536   C. 537   D. 538   E. 539

Answer ☐

Question 29

One side of a rectangle is 12cm. If the area of the rectangle is 84cm², what is the length of shorter side?

A. 5cm   B. 6cm   C. 7cm   D. 8cm   E. 9cm

Answer ☐

Question 30

A rectangle has an area of 8cm². The length of one side is 2cm. What is the perimeter?

A. 4cm   B. 6cm   C. 8cm   D. 10cm   E. None of these.

Answer ☐

Now that you have completed the sample numeracy test work through your answers carefully before moving onto the next section of the guide.

ANSWERS TO NUMERICAL NUMERACY TEST

1. C		**16.** B	
2. A		**17.** A	
3. D		**18.** C	
4. E		**19.** E	
5. B		**20.** C	
6. D		**21.** C	
7. A		**22.** E	
8. E		**23.** B	
9. A		**24.** D	
10. B		**25.** A	
11. B		**26.** B	
12. C		**27.** A	
13. C		**28.** E	
14. D		**29.** C	
15. E		**30.** E	

NUMERICAL TESTS - SPEED, DISTANCE AND TIME

Depending on the technicality of the position you are applying for, you may be required to answers questions that are based on speed, distance and time. Questions of this nature are usually utilised during selection processes for air traffic controller positions and some Armed Forces jobs.

Accuracy and agility in speed, distance, and time calculations will help you perform well during the assessment. The following information will assist you in understanding how to tackle these types of question. Even if you are not required to sit this type of test during your psychometric assessment they are still excellent practice for improving your ability in numerical reasoning.

When trying to solve these problems it is important to consider three variables: speed, distance and time. Try not to get too worried as two of these variables will always be known. The easiest way to solve these equations is to use the following formulas:

$$Speed = \frac{Distance}{Time}$$

$$Distance = Speed \times Time$$

$$Time = \frac{Distance}{Speed}$$

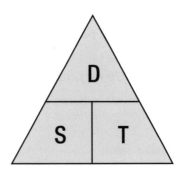

The triangular diagram above is ideal for helping you to remember the formula. Simply place your finger over the variable you are trying to discover, you will then see the equation required.

For example if you wanted to obtain the time, placing your finger on 'T' would show that you would need to *divide* distance (D) by speed (S).

Let's now work through some examples:

1. A train travels 60 miles in 3 hours. What is the train's speed?

> *Formula: Speed = distance ÷ time*
>
> Speed = 60 ÷ 3 = **20 mph**

2. A car is travelling at 30 mph for 70 minutes. What is the distance travelled?

With this problem it is important to remember to work in minutes!

So, 30 mph = 0.5 miles per minute (30 ÷ 60)

70 (minutes) × 0.5 = **35 miles**

You can use the formula but you need to convert the minutes into hours and remember that 0.1 = 1/10 of 60 minutes:

Formula: Distance = speed × time

Distance = 30 × 1.1666r (1 hour 10 mins) = **35**

3. A tank is driving at 48 mph over 60 miles. How long was it driving for?

Formula: Time =distance ÷ speed

Time = 60 ÷ 48 = **1 hour 15 minutes**

Take these steps

I. You know that 48 mph = 48 miles in 60 minutes.

II. The difference between 60 and 48 is 12, which is ¼ of 48.

III. You can then take ¼ of 60, which gives 15 minutes, and add that to 60 minutes = 75 minutes.

IV. Then convert to hours = 1 hour 15 minutes for the answer!

OR

Take these steps

I. You know that 48 mph = 0.8 miles per minute.

II. 60 ÷ 0.8 = 75 minutes.

III. Convert into hours = 1 hour 15 minutes.

Once you understand how to calculate speed, distance and time, take your time to work through the 30 sample test questions.

SAMPLE SPEED, DISTANCE AND TIME TEST QUESTIONS

(Give all distances and speeds in whole numbers)

Question 1

You are travelling at 28mph for 75 minutes. How far do you travel?

Answer

Question 2

You travel 15 miles in half an hour. What speed are you travelling at?

Answer

Question 3

You travel 33 miles at a constant speed of 55mph. How long are you travelling for?

Answer

Question 4

You are travelling at 75 mph for 1 and half hours. How far do you travel?

Answer

Question 5

You travel 61 miles in 1 hour and 5 minutes. What speed are you travelling at?

Answer

Question 6

You travel 90 miles at a constant speed of 30 mph. How long are you travelling for?

Answer

Question 7

You are travelling at 70mph for 125 minutes. How far do you travel?

Answer

Question 8

You travel 2.5 miles in 5 minutes. What speed are you travelling at?

Answer

Question 9

You travel 75 miles at a constant speed of 45mph. How long are you travelling for?

Answer

Question 10

You are travelling at 59 mph for quarter of an hour. How far do you travel?

Answer

Question 11

You travel 325 miles in 4 hours and 6 minutes. What speed are you travelling at?

Answer

Question 12

You travel 38 miles at 45 mph. How long are you travelling for?

Answer

Question 13

You are travelling at 80 mph for 15 minutes. How far do you travel?

Answer

Question 14

You travel 63 miles in 56 minutes. What speed are you travelling at?

Answer

Question 15

You travel 18 miles at 50 mph. How long are you travelling for?

Answer

Question 16

You are travelling at 65 mph for one hour and 10 minutes. How far do you travel?

Answer

Question 17

You travel 120 miles in two hours. What speed are you travelling at?

Answer

Question 18

You travel 80 miles at 50 mph. How long are you travelling for?

Answer

Question 19

You are travelling at 40 mph for half an hour. How far do you travel?

Answer

Question 20

You travel 80 miles in 1¾ of an hour. What speed are you travelling at?

Answer

Question 21

You travel 35 miles at 70 mph. How long are you travelling for?

Answer

Question 22
You are travelling at 15 mph for 8 minutes. How far do you travel?

Answer

Question 23
You travel 16 miles in quarter of an hour. What speed are you travelling at?

Answer

Question 24
You travel 60 miles at 55 mph. How long are you travelling for?

Answer

Question 25
You are travelling at 30 mph for 10 minutes. How far do you travel?

Answer

Question 26
You travel 75 miles in one and half hours. What speed are you travelling at?

Answer

Question 27
You travel 1 mile at 60 mph. How long are you travelling for?

Answer

Question 28
You are travelling at 50 mph for 2 and half hours. How far do you travel?

Answer

Question 29

You travel 100 miles in 1 hour and 55 minutes. What speed are you travelling at?

Answer ☐

Question 30

You travel 600 miles at 80 mph. How long are you travelling for?

Answer ☐

ANSWERS TO SPEED, DISTANCE AND TIME TEST

1. 35 miles

2. 30 mph

3. 36 mins

4. 112.5 miles

5. 56 mph

6. 3 hours

7. 146 miles

8. 30 mph

9. 1hour 40 minutes

10. 14.75 miles

11. 79 mph

12. 51 mins

13. 20 miles

14. 14.75 miles

15. 21 minutes and 36 seconds

16. 75.833 rounded up to 76 miles

17. 60mph

18. 1 hour 36 mins

19. 20 miles

20. 45.7 mph

21. 30 mins

22. 2 miles

23. 64 mph

24. 1 hour 5 mins

25. 5 miles

26. 50 mph

27. 1 minute

28. 125 miles

29. 52 mph

30. 7 hours 30 minutes

You can practice FREE speed, distance and time test questions at:
SpeedDistanceTime.info

CHAPTER 3
SPATIAL REASONING TEST

For jobs and careers that involve a practical element to them, you may be required to sit what is called a 'spatial reasoning' test.

The definition of spatial reasoning is as follows:

'The ability to interpret and make drawings from mental images and visualise movement or change in those images.'

Let us take a look at a sample question.

Example question

Take a look at the following 3 shapes. Note the letters on the side of each shape:

Join all of the 3 shapes together with the corresponding letters to make the following shape:

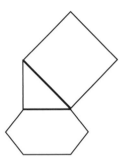

During the following spatial reasoning exercise your task is to look at the given shapes and decide which of the examples matches the shape when joined together by the corresponding letters. You have 3 minutes to answer the 8 questions.

SPATIAL REASONING TEST 1

Question 1

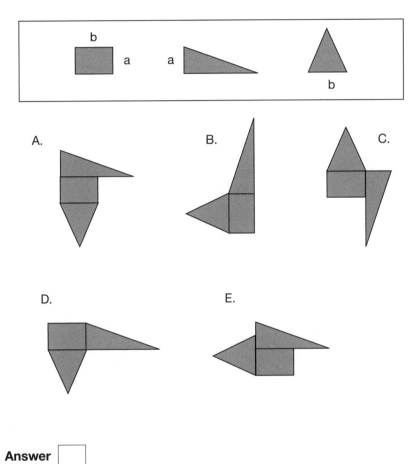

Answer

Question 2

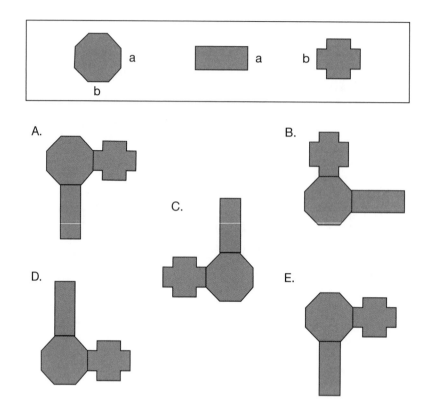

Answer ☐

Question 3

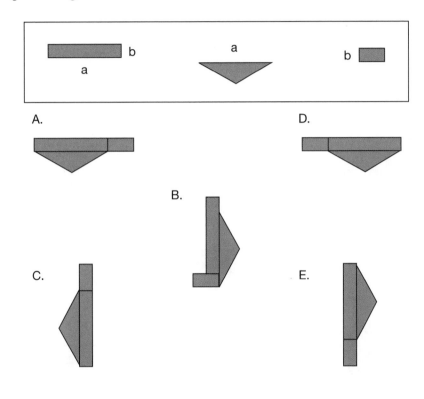

A.

D.

B.

C.

E.

Answer ☐

Question 4

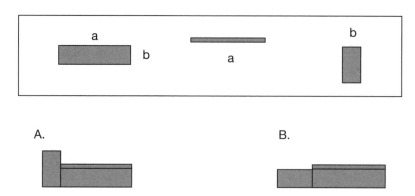

A.

B.

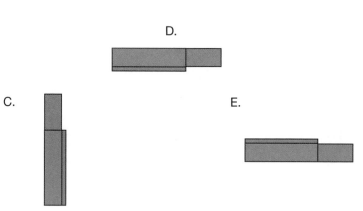

D.

C.

E.

Answer ☐

Question 5

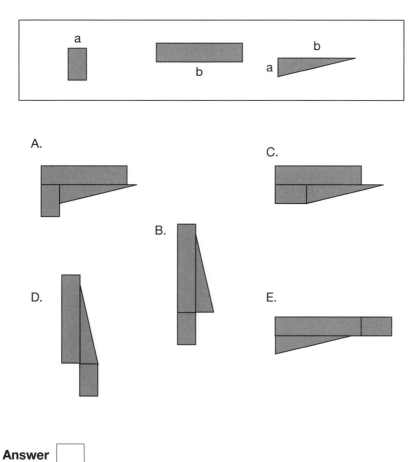

Answer [ ]

Question 6

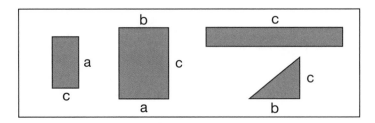

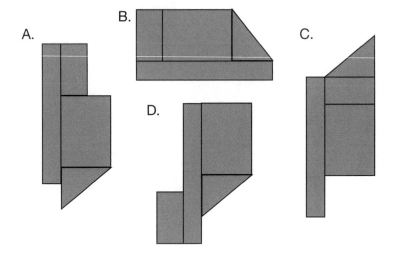

Answer ☐

Question 7

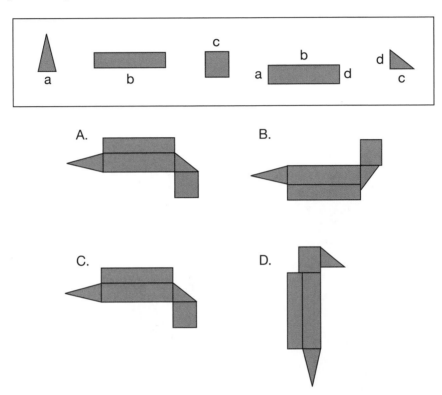

Answer ☐

Question 8

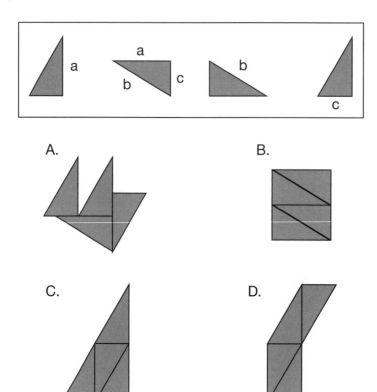

A.

B.

C.

D.

Answer ☐

Now that you have completed the exercise take the time to work through your answers carefully. If you got any incorrect, make sure you understand how the correct answer is reached as this will assist you during your development.

ANSWERS TO SPATIAL REASONING TEST 1

1. B

2. D

3. A

4. E

5. D

6. B

7. A

8. C

SPATIAL REASONING TEST 2

During the second spatial reasoning test that I've provided you with you will be required to look at 3-dimensional objects. You have to imagine the 3-dimensional objects rotated in a specific way and then match them up against a choice of examples.

Look at the 2 objects below:

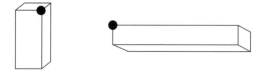

You now have to decide which of the 4 options provided demonstrates both objects rotated with the dot in the correct position. Look at the options below:

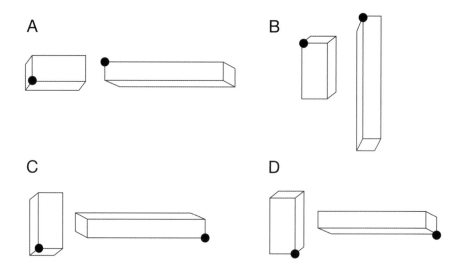

The correct answer is C

Now move on to spatial reasoning test exercise 2. You have 3 minutes in which to complete the 8 questions.

Question 1

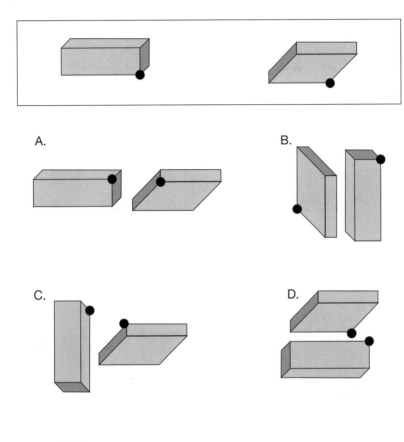

Answer ☐

Question 2

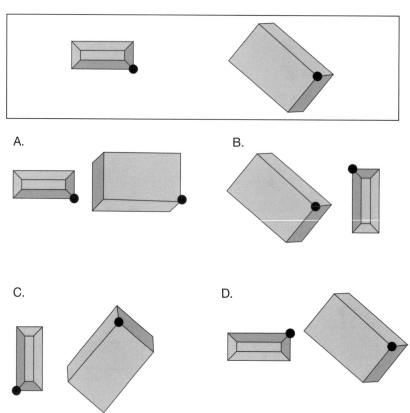

A.

B.

C.

D.

Answer

Question 3

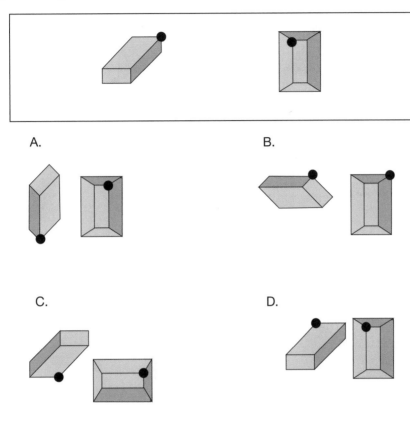

A.

B.

C.

D.

Answer ☐

Question 4

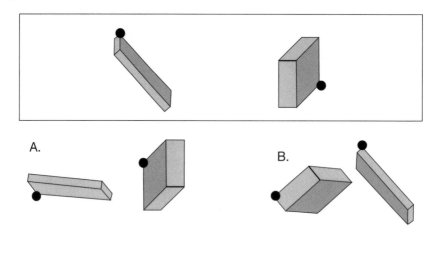

A.

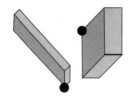

B.

C.

D.

Answer ☐

Question 5

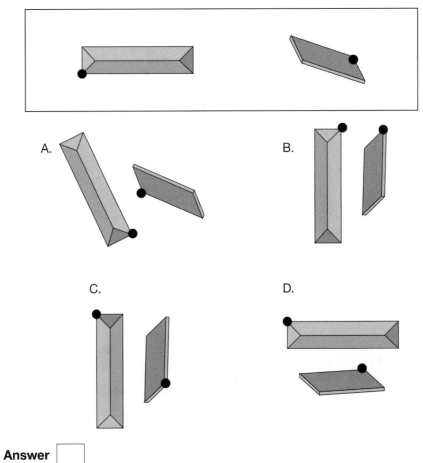

A.

B.

C.

D.

Answer ☐

Question 6

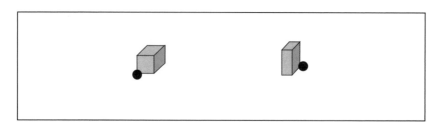

A.

B.

C.

D.

Answer

Question 7

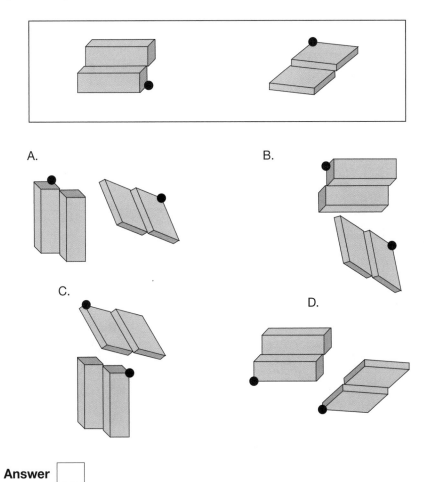

Answer ☐

Question 8

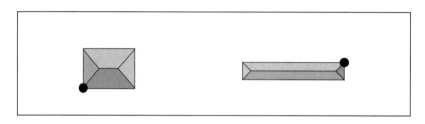

A.

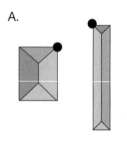

B.

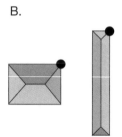

C.

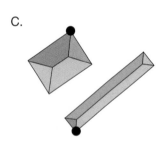

D.

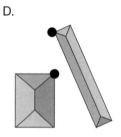

Answer

ANSWERS TO SPATIAL REASONING TEST EXERCISE 2

1. B

2. C

3. C

4. C

5. A

6. B

7. B

8. C

CHAPTER 4
WORK RATE TESTS AND CONCENTRATION TESTS

Some assessors will want to see evidence of how effective you are at carrying out routine tasks and also how good you are at concentrating for long periods of time.

During this chapter I will provide you with a large number of sample test questions that will go a long way to helping you to improve in these areas. To begin with we will take a look at 'work rate' tests.

WORK RATE TESTS

This form of test assesses your ability to work quickly and accurately whilst carrying out routine tasks. Before we move on to the test questions, let's take a look at a sample question. To begin with, study the following box which contains different numbers, letters and symbols.

5	6	3	1	2	NUMBERS
J	F	T	S	W	LETTERS
◣	✚	☾	⬠	●	SYMBOLS

COLUMNS

In the sample questions that I have provided you with, you will be given a code consisting of numbers, letters or symbols. Your task is to look at the 5 provided alternative codes and decide which one has been taken from the SAME columns as the original code.

For example, take a look at the following code:

CODE A – 563

Now look at the 5 alternatives, which are taken from the above grid and decide which code has been taken from the same columns as code A.

A. J ☾ 2   B. ◣ FT   C. ✚ 51   D. ● 6S   E. 3J2

You can see that the answer is in fact B and the code ◣ FT. The reason for this is that this code has been taken from the **same columns** and in the **same order** as the original code.

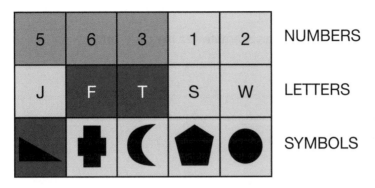

NUMBERS

LETTERS

SYMBOLS

COLUMNS

ORIGINAL CODE

MATCHING CODE

Now take the time to work through the following exercises. You have 10 minutes to work through the 15 questions. If you do not finish the test, try practising the questions you have missed in your own time. If you get any wrong, make sure you go back and understand why.

Question 1

Which of the answers below is an alternative to the code **765**?

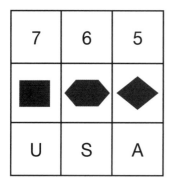

A. U ⬛ 5   **B.** U ● S   **C.** ◆ 6U   **D.** US ◆

Answer ☐

Question 2

Which of the answers below is an alternative to the code **A8** ?

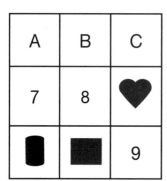

A. ▮ C9   **B.** 78 ▬   **C.** 7B9   **D.** 897

Answer ☐

Question 3

Which of the answers below is an alternative to the code **YEF**?

F	Y	E	W
▲	▶	▼	◀
2	4	8	1

A. 4 ▼ 1   **B.** ▶ 84   **C.** 481   **D.** ▶ ▼ 2

Answer [ ]

Question 4

Which of the answers below is an alternative to the code **178**?

A	B	C	Z
7	8	3	1
▼	▶	◀	▲

A. ▲ A3   **B.** Z ▼ 3   **C.** ▲ AB   **D.** ▶ 3Z

Answer [ ]

Question 5

Which of the answers below is an alternative to the code **82T**?

S	2	T	8
★	◗	⌒	✦
W	4	6	Q

A. ✦4W   **B.** Q4★   **C.** Q4 ⌒   **D.** ◗S4

Answer [   ]

Question 6

Which of the answers below is an alternative to the code **X39**?

D	S	E	X
9	3	2	5
0	1	4	8

A. 514   **B.** 8S2   **C.** 0S8   **D.** 51D

Answer [   ]

Question 7

Which of the answers below is an alternative to the code **XWQ**?

■	●	▲	O
S	7	3	8
Q	X	W	K

A. 73 ● **B.** 37K **C.** O SX **D.** ● 3 ■

Answer ⬚

Question 8

Which of the answers below is an alternative to the code **482**?

I	B	N	M
8	7	4	2
▲	●	O	■

A. NIM **B.** NBI **C.** 7 O 2 **D.** ● MN

Answer ⬚

Question 9

Which of the answers below is an alternative to the code **0W9**?

4	0	2	9
S	8	3	8
Q	X	W	K

A. X3Q   **B.** 7X8   **C.** QS4   **D.** X28

Answer [   ]

Question 10

Which of the answers below is an alternative to the code **672**?

U	Z	R	E
8	7	4	2
6	3	5	1

A. U31   **B.** 6Z4   **C.** 8Z5   **D.** 3E8

Answer [   ]

Question 11

Which of the answers below is an alternative to the code **3PJ**?

R	A	F	P
1	2	3	4
J	■	D	●

A. D ● A   **B.** 14F   **C.** ■ R3   **D.** D41

Answer

Question 12

Which of the answers below is an alternative to the code **72S**?

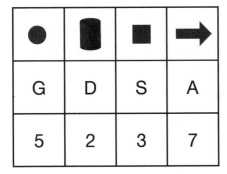

●	▮	■	→
G	D	S	A
5	2	3	7

A. SD ➡   **B.** AD3   **C.** 52 ■   **D.** A3D

Answer

Question 13

Which of the answers below is an alternative to the code **1LS**?

R	A	F	P
J	S	2	4
●	H	■	L
1	▮	3	➡

A. RPF   **B.** P4 ➡   **C.** ● 4 ▮   **D.** RAF

Answer [ ]

Question 14

Which of the answers below is an alternative to the code **X1W3D**?

G	D	S	A	W	L
5	2	3	7	0	1
X	Y	Z	Q	E	T

A. 51WZX   **B.** Y1QZT   **C.** GTEZY   **D.** YZ7SD

Answer [ ]

Question 15

Which of the answers below is an alternative to the code **J4F**?

R		F	P
J			4
	H		L
1		3	

A. 1HF   **B.** RPL   **C.** 31P   **D.** 1L3

Answer

ANSWERS TO WORK RATE TEST 1

1.	D	**9.**	D
2.	C	**10.**	A
3.	D	**11.**	D
4.	C	**12.**	B
5.	C	**13.**	C
6.	D	**14.**	C
7.	D	**15.**	D
8.	A		

CONCENTRATION TEST PART 1

As previously stated during this chapter, many technical posts will require you to sit some form of concentration test. These tests are a lot harder than they first appear.

During the first type of test I am going to show you, you will be required to view a sequence of letters. Let's assume that the sequence of letters looks like the following. Please note that during the real test the letters may appear on a computer screen and also individually over a set period of time, as opposed to collectively as per below.

W	E	Q	X	R	E

You are required to study the above sequence of letters for one minute only. Once the minute is up, cover the above sequence with your hand or a sheet of paper, and answer the following questions:

Question 1

How many letter E's were there in the sequence?

Answer [ ]

Question 2

How many letters were there in between the letter W and the letter X?

Answer [ ]

Question 3

What letter was between the letter Q and the letter R?

Answer [ ]

ANSWERS TO SAMPLE TEST QUESTIONS

1. Two

2. Two

3. X

Hopefully you managed to get the questions correct. Your ability to successfully pass this test will be dependant on how good your memory is. In order to improve your ability during this test try the following sample exercise.

CONCENTRATION TEST 1

R	A	L	E	S	S

Study the above sequence of letters for one minute only. Once the minute is up, cover the above sequence with your hand or a sheet of paper, and answer the following questions:

Question 1

How many letter S's were in the sequence?

Answer [　　　]

Question 2

How many letters were there in between the letter R and the letter E?

Answer [　　　]

Question 3

What was the first letter in the sequence?

Answer [　　　]

CONCENTRATION TEST 2

F	A	Q	A	Q	S

Study the above sequence of letters for one minute only. Once the minute is up, cover the above sequence with your hand or a sheet of paper, and answer the following questions:

Question 1

How many letters were there in the entire sequence?

Answer

Question 2

How many letters were there in between the letter F and the letter S?

Answer

Question 3

What was the third letter in the sequence?

Answer

CONCENTRATION TEST 3

E	X	Q	E	E	W	Z

Study the above sequence of letters for one minute only. Once the minute is up, cover the above sequence with your hand or a sheet of paper, and answer the following questions:

Question 1

How many letters were there in the entire sequence?

Answer

Question 2

How many letter E's were there in the sequence?

Answer

Question 3

How many letters were there in between the letter Q and the letter W?

Answer

CONCENTRATION TEST 4

Y	t	d	D	w	W	g

Study the above sequence of letters for one minute only. Once the minute is up, cover the above sequence with your hand or a sheet of paper, and answer the following questions:

Question 1

How many capital letters were there in the sequence?

Answer

Question 2

How many lower case (non capital) letters were there in the sequence?

Answer

Question 3

How many letters were there in between the letter t and the letter g?

Answer

CONCENTRATION TEST 5

S	k	T	t	Y	U	T	t

Study the above sequence of letters for one minute only. Once the minute is up, cover the above sequence with your hand or a sheet of paper, and answer the following questions:

Question 1

How many capital letters were there in the sequence?

Answer _____

Question 2

How many letters were there in the entire sequence?

Answer _____

Question 3

How many capital letters were there in between the letter k and the letter U?

Answer _____

CONCENTRATION TEST 6

x	c	o	y	L	t	G	g

Study the above sequence of letters for one minute only. Once the minute is up, cover the above sequence with your hand or a sheet of paper, and answer the following questions:

Question 1

How many lower case (non capital) letters were there in the sequence?

Answer [   ]

Question 2

How many letters were there between the letter x and the letter G?

Answer [   ]

Question 3

How many lower case (non capital) letters were there in between the letter x and the letter G?

Answer [   ]

CONCENTRATION TEST 7

p	y	T	t	R

Study the above sequence of letters for one minute only. Once the minute is up, cover the above sequence with your hand or a sheet of paper, and answer the following questions:

Question 1

How many capital letters were there in the sequence?

Answer

Question 2

How many capital letters were there between the letter y and the letter R?

Answer

Question 3

What was the fourth letter in the sequence?

Answer

CONCENTRATION TEST 8

O	Q	s	S	A	a	G

Study the above sequence of letters for one minute only. Once the minute is up, cover the above sequence with your hand or a sheet of paper, and answer the following questions:

Question 1

How many capital letters were there in the sequence?

Answer [   ]

Question 2

What were the fifth and sixth letters in the sequence?

Answer [   ]

Question 3

What was the last letter in the sequence?

Answer [   ]

CONCENTRATION TEST 9

t	t	r	S	W	t	Q

Study the above sequence of letters for one minute only. Once the minute is up, cover the above sequence with your hand or a sheet of paper, and answer the following questions:

Question 1

Which letter appears the most times in the sequence?

Answer

Question 2

What was the fifth letter in the sequence?

Answer

Question 3

Which two letters appear between the letter S and the letter Q?

Answer

CONCENTRATION TEST 10

v	b	n	q	w	A	s	s	d

Study the above sequence of letters for one minute only. Once the minute is up, cover the above sequence with your hand or a sheet of paper, and answer the following questions:

Question 1

How many letters were there in the sequence?

Answer

Question 2

What was the third letter in the sequence?

Answer

Question 3

Which letter appears the most in the sequence?

Answer

ANSWERS TO CONCENTRATION TESTS

CONCENTRATION TEST 1

1. 2

2. 2

3. R

CONCENTRATION TEST 2

1. 6

2. 4

3. Q

CONCENTRATION TEST 3

1. 7

2. 3

3. 2

CONCENTRATION TEST 4

1. 3

2. 4

3. 4

CONCENTRATION TEST 5

1. 5

2. 8

3. 2

CONCENTRATION TEST 6

1. 6

2. 5

3. 4

CONCENTRATION TEST 7

1. 2

2. 1

3. t

CONCENTRATION TEST 8

1. 5

2. A + a

3. G

CONCENTRATION TEST 9

1. t

2. W

3. W + t

CONCENTRATION TEST 10

1. 9

2. n

3. s

CONCENTRATION TEST PART 2

During the second part of my concentration test you will be required to view a number of different grids which contain coloured squares. Each grid will appear individually. Once the sequence of grids has disappeared you will be required to state which pattern the collective coloured squares make up from a number of different options.

Take a look at the following four grids for 5 seconds only:

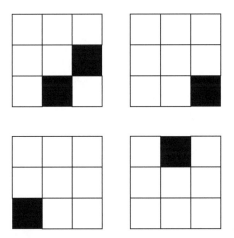

Once you have studied the grids for 5 seconds cover them with a sheet of paper. Now decide from the following four options which grid contains the collective group of coloured squares from the four grids.

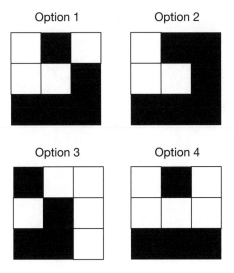

As you will see, **Option 1** accurately reflects the combined locations of the coloured squares from the initial four grids.

Once you understand what is required, move on to the following exercises.

QUESTION 1

Study the following grids for 5 seconds only. Then turn the page and decide from the four options available which grid contains the collective group of coloured squares from the grids.

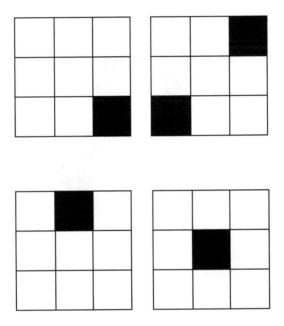

QUESTION 1 OPTIONS

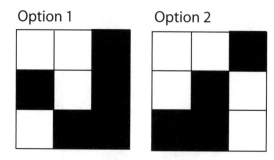

Option 1   Option 2

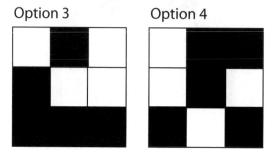

Option 3   Option 4

Answer

QUESTION 2

Study the following grids for 5 seconds only. Then turn the page and decide from the four options available which grid contains the collective group of coloured squares from the grids.

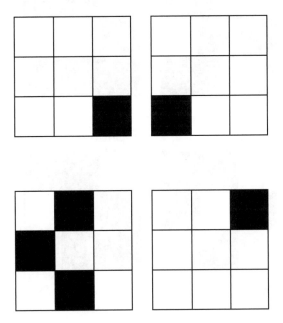

QUESTION 2 OPTIONS

Option 1   Option 2

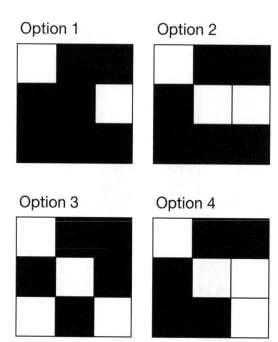

Option 3   Option 4

Answer ▢

QUESTION 3

Study the following grids for 5 seconds only. Then turn the page and decide from the four options available which grid contains the collective group of coloured squares from the grids.

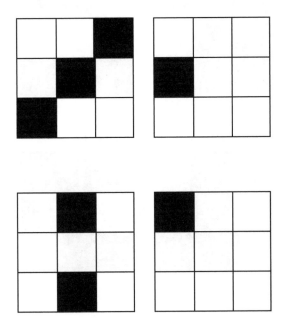

QUESTION 3 OPTIONS

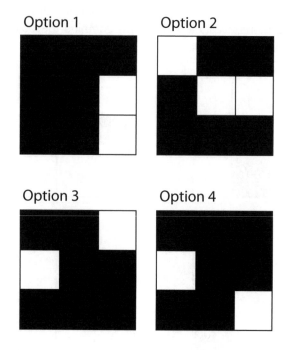

Option 1   Option 2

Option 3   Option 4

Answer [   ]

QUESTION 4

Study the following grids for 5 seconds only. Then turn the page and decide from the four options available which grid contains the collective group of coloured squares from the grids.

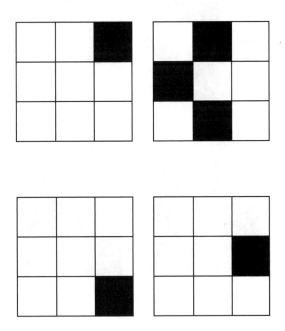

QUESTION 4 OPTIONS

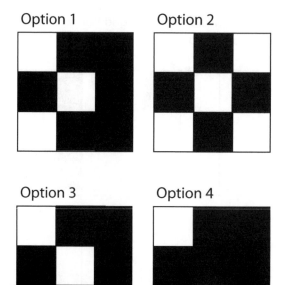

| Option 1 | Option 2 |

| Option 3 | Option 4 |

Answer

QUESTION 5

Study the following grids for 5 seconds only. Then turn the page and decide from the four options available which grid contains the collective group of coloured squares from the grids.

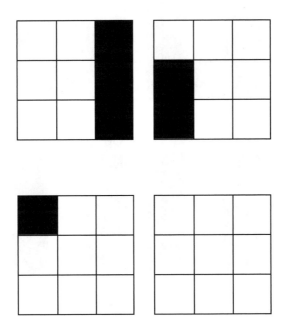

QUESTION 5 OPTIONS

Option 1   **Option 2**

Option 3   **Option 4**

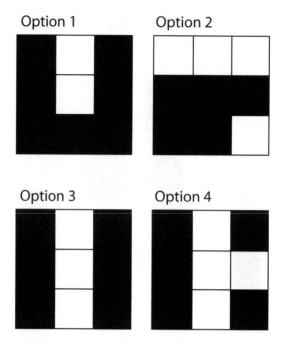

Answer [   ]

QUESTION 6

Study the following grids for 5 seconds only. Then turn the page and decide from the four options available which grid contains the collective group of coloured squares from the grids.

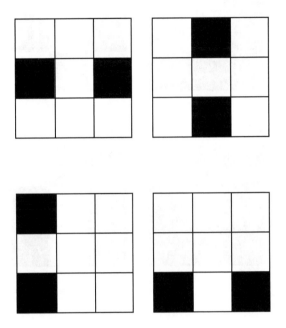

QUESTION 6 OPTIONS

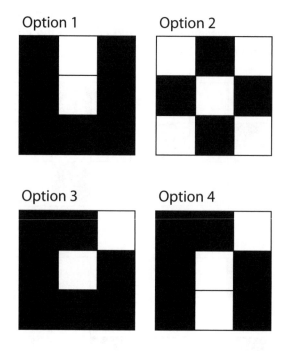

Option 1   Option 2

Option 3   Option 4

Answer [ ]

QUESTION 7

Study the following grids for 5 seconds only. Then turn the page and decide from the four options available which grid contains the collective group of coloured squares from the grids.

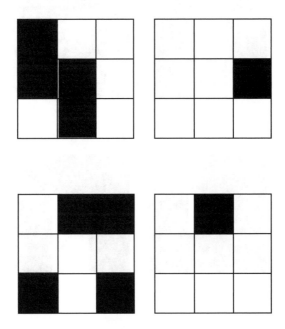

QUESTION 7 OPTIONS

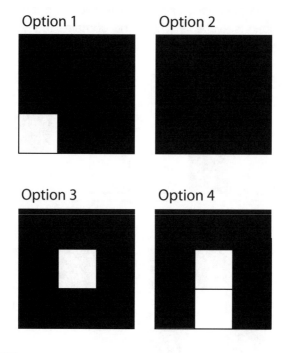

Answer ☐

QUESTION 8

Study the following grids for 5 seconds only. Then turn the page and decide from the four options available which grid contains the collective group of coloured squares from the grids.

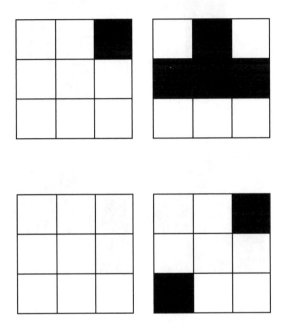

QUESTION 8 OPTIONS

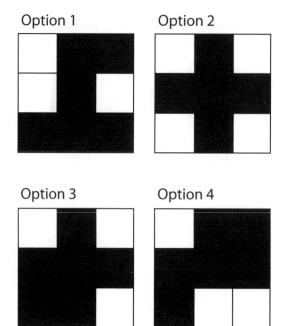

Option 1   Option 2

Option 3   Option 4

Answer [   ]

QUESTION 9

Study the following grids for 5 seconds only. Then turn the page and decide from the four options available which grid contains the collective group of coloured squares from the grids.

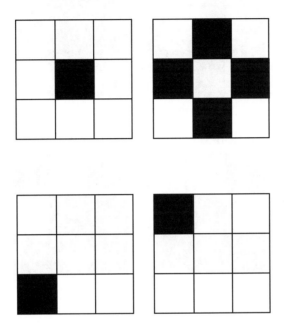

QUESTION 9 OPTIONS

Option 1

Option 2

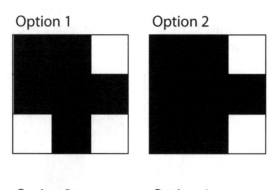

Option 3

Option 4

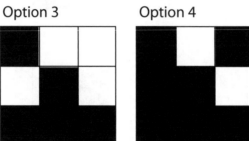

Answer

QUESTION 10

Study the following grids for 5 seconds only. Then turn the page and decide from the four options available which grid contains the collective group of coloured squares from the grids.

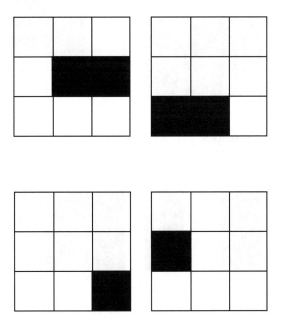

QUESTION 7 OPTIONS

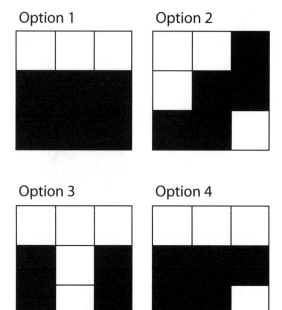

Option 1

Option 2

Option 3

Option 4

Answer

ANSWERS TO CONCENTRATION TEST PART 2

1. Option 4
2. Option 2
3. Option 1
4. Option 1
5. Option 3
6. Option 3
7. Option 2
8. Option 4
9. Option 2
10. Option 1

CONCENTRATION TEST PART 3

The next type of concentration test is designed to assess your ability to concentrate whilst performing tasks at high speed. I have found this type of test to be excellent for improving overall concentration abilities whilst performing psychometric tests.

In the tests that follow you will be presented with rows of numbers, letters or dots. Your task is to decide how many types of specific letters there are in each row or how many groupings of dots there are in the sequence.

SAMPLE TEST QUESTIONS

Take a look at the following row of *letters* and decide how many capital letters **R** there are in the sequence.

The answer is 4.

Now take a look at the following row of dots and decide how many boxes contain 4 dots only:

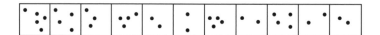

You will notice that the 2nd, 4th, 7th and 9th boxes each contain 4 dots as follows:

You will notice that I have placed a single diagonal line through each of the boxes that contains 4 dots.

On the following pages I have provided you with ten sample concentration tests. During the first set of five concentration tests you are required to locate specific letters and/or numbers that are contained within rows and columns. Full instructions are provided at the start of each test.

During the second set of five concentration tests you will be required to search for groups of 4 dots in rows and columns of boxes. Once again, full instructions are provided.

CONCENTRATION TEST 1

Cross out the letter 'R' (upper case) in each row. Write down the total number that you cross out in each row in the box provided at the end of each row. You have 60 seconds to complete the test.

1.	Q	r	R	g	y	U	h	J	R	j	R	k	L	B	n	
2.	R	R	R	v	B	n	M	U	u	d	f	O	p	T	R	
3.	C	x	X	F	R	G	t	p	A	R	f	V	R	y	U	
4.	Q	R	R	t	G	N	H	J	r	r	F	P	F	R	r	
5.	Q	a	Z	x	R	t	I	o	M	B	R	D	x	A	S	
6.	R	s	a	A	e	E	R	C	Y	U	r	j	P	o	R	
7.	T	R	r	P	F	r	S	N	b	V	c	F	F	R	R	
8.	G	v	R	r	R	y	R	P	R	r	D	e	E	R	F	
9.	T	R	K	P	o	u	b	g	t	m	R	r	X	r	R	
10.	C	B	n	h	j	Y	I	p	R	R	R	r	R	C	d	
11.	R	R	r	Y	u	B	v	M	n	h	K	j	R	E	R	
12.	A	W	r	E	R	f	p	U	I	H	R	y	U	B	R	
13.	R	r	Q	q	B	G	R	t	Q	w	E	F	T	y	R	
14.	T	R	A	I	N	D	P	I	V	E	R	D	T	y	S	
15.	d	x	z	Z	R	n	K	i	i	R	r	R	O	p	o	
16.	Q	R	r	E	D	D	e	w	K	i	I	O	P	R	R	
17.	H	O	w	B	e	E	R	r	R	R	V	R	H	j	R	
18.	K	j	u	U	Y	i	Y	r	R	R	D	X	z	q	Q	
19.	P	y	g	h	j	I	r	t	r	e	R	e	R	q	Z	
20.	B	h	B	h	r	r	R	r	N	B	H	y	Y	R	F	

CONCENTRATION TEST 2

Cross out the letter 'o' (lower case). Write down the total number that you cross out in each row in the box provided at the end of each row. You have 60 seconds to complete the test.

1.	o	O	t	Q	w	q	O	o	A	B	u	U	o	o	O	
2.	O	o	g	Y	t	B	c	C	c	O	o	o	o	D	w	
3.	B	o	O	g	a	s	S	q	Q	t	Q	q	O	o	G	
4.	I	L	N	h	U	u	O	o	H	y	t	R	o	O	o	
5.	G	V	v	R	t	Y	o	o	P	i	O	O	o	O	R	
6.	G	t	y	U	J	P	p	O	o	D	d	O	o	S	Q	
7.	O	o	O	o	o	o	Y	t	Y	q	Q	q	o	c	c	
8.	I	u	V	c	c	F	r	d	w	H	y	h	u	o	o	
9.	Y	o	o	U	o	O	O	y	D	e	q	A	q	O	o	
10.	R	r	t	o	u	y	G	b	t	r	e	o	o	o	P	
11.	o	O	c	o	d	d	D	O	c	c	O	o	o	d	R	
12.	B	v	c	f	R	o	y	f	D	r	d	r	a	A	a	
13.	F	t	t	t	d	r	e	o	o	p	u	o	Q	t	r	
14.	F	g	r	t	y	N	H	N	h	o	p	O	o	I	y	
15.	T	r	e	d	w	o	u	i	y	F	c	r	D	e	W	
16.	o	o	O	o	p	O	u	i	S	t	d	r	s	S	O	
17.	I	o	O	A	a	a	c	C	c	g	o	o	o	R	t	
18.	G	g	g	g	o	t	f	d	r	t	u	u	o	o	j	
19.	Q	c	v	b	g	t	y	u	O	o	O	o	G	y	c	
20.	K	I	o	i	u	y	t	r	e	o	u	y	o	j	h	

CONCENTRATION TEST 3

Cross out the letters 'w' (lower case) and 'V' (upper case). Search for both of these letters at the same time. Write down the total combined number that you cross out in each row in the box provided at the end of each row. You have 60 seconds to complete the test.

1.	v	W	w	V	e	w	h	j	U	i	X	x	W	w	v	
2.	V	u	U	w	G	t	y	u	W	w	V	v	W	o	o	
3.	W	W	V	V	v	v	w	w	y	u	i	p	v	W	W	
4.	V	g	h	j	K	O	p	t	Y	V	v	W	W	w	V	
5.	Y	U	u	u	v	v	W	M	m	w	e	V	v	N	n	
6.	q	q	Q	G	g	H	Y	u	i	R	T	y	V	w	v	
7.	V	y	u	Y	u	o	p	N	h	j	W	w	V	V	v	
8.	t	y	m	k	m	N	b	C	x	W	w	V	v	b	v	
9.	O	o	V	v	f	g	h	j	k	n	h	N	h	V	X	
10.	T	V	v	X	c	d	W	w	W	v	V	v	f	r	p	
11.	V	V	v	w	W	w	v	V	v	W	w	g	y	Y	v	
12.	R	t	y	u	i	B	g	v	f	r	D	r	Q	w	W	
13.	R	t	y	V	c	V	c	v	f	r	W	w	W	w	V	
14.	G	y	u	i	O	p	R	t	y	E	w	V	V	v	W	
15.	Y	Y	y	Y	X	v	W	W	w	w	r	t	y	u	v	
16.	W	w	w	v	t	u	i	n	h	v	V	w	W	w	f	
17.	r	t	y	y	u	i	V	b	n	h	g	w	w	W	w	
18.	i	o	q	w	S	S	X	W	V	Z	z	V	v	W	y	
19.	P	o	Y	u	i	V	v	X	w	W	w	R	t	R	y	
20.	y	u	V	x	s	t	Y	u	y	W	w	C	d	V	w	

CONCENTRATION TEST 4

Cross out the number 8 and the letter 'b' (lower case). Search for both letter and number at the same time. Write down the total combined number that you cross out in each row in the box provided at the end of each row. You have 60 seconds to complete the test.

1.	8	B	8	V	v	W	q	P	p	r	g	B	b	8	u	
2.	B	b	R	r	r	y	U	i	8	8	B	B	b	g	G	
3.	j	u	p	P	b	v	f	r	B	b	w	3	6	7	R	
4.	8	3	2	h	y	U	x	W	w	v	x	v	b	B	8	
5.	f	G	g	B	p	h	b	b	b	B	B	8	8	5	3	
6.	y	u	U	7	6	5	8	e	r	d	r	w	8	B	b	
7.	o	O	o	P	7	8	5	b	3	8	3	R	r	S	I	
8.	B	b	3	8	B	B	b	h	h	V	c	b	B	7	1	
9.	1	3	c	V	f	I	u	y	t	r	B	b	8	8	8	
10.	y	B	b	8	4	3	3	3	X	x	x	f	F	r	t	
11.	Q	q	H	b	B	b	8	B	6	3	3	2	u	B	b	
12.	G	G	g	B	b	8	3	8	3	D	d	D	I	P	p	
13.	G	b	b	8	8	6	5	4	0	L	o	P	p	P	B	
14.	3	B	b	8	3	B	B	b	3	E	e	3	8	4	P	
15.	t	Y	y	D	e	e	D	f	g	W	8	8	P	P	B	
16.	C	C	b	n	B	8	B	8	B	b	8	3	9	3	9	
17.	6	6	b	B	8	8	d	k	I	p	o	U	S	y	Y	
18.	P	p	8	F	d	D	c	C	8	B	b	8	f	F	f	
19.	8	8	C	f	z	s	W	w	R	r	T	8	3	B	b	
20.	H	y	y	b	B	8	8	8	H	H	h	D	r	e	W	

CONCENTRATION TEST 5

Cross out the letter 'e' (lower case) and the number '3'. Search for both letter and number at the same time. Write down the number crossed out in the box provided at the end of each row. You have 60 seconds to complete the test.

1.	E	6	e	8	8	e	3	p	b	d	e	E	3	8	T	
2.	e	8	3	6	7	y	u	I	V	f	E	e	b	B	E	
3.	W	w	q	D	d	c	X	z	O	p	e	R	6	8	3	
4.	y	u	I	o	p	P	t	T	Y	e	E	3	8	6	F	
5.	g	B	4	3	2	7	8	3	e	E	3	4	E	e	3	
6.	e	3	3	e	E	d	W	q	h	j	K	8	7	N	9	
7.	3	e	E	8	B	8	3	e	E	k	K	3	e	8	7	
8.	f	C	x	b	g	t	T	r	6	8	3	4	X	d	e	
9.	3	3	3	b	8	b	e	3	E	3	8	3	4	0	1	
10.	e	E	j	H	g	b	3	E	e	3	w	b	V	v	E	
11.	8	3	B	v	C	f	v	e	8	4	3	3	3	e	v	
12.	6	7	8	v	c	D	f	3	7	8	6	E	e	e	V	
13.	e	3	e	3	E	8	E	3	e	E	3	2	8	G	g	
14.	7	y	h	n	g	f	d	e	E	4	E	e	3	D	d	
15.	k	I	L	j	h	y	V	v	8	4	2	b	V	v	E	
16.	g	Y	y	i	9	8	7	0	3	O	o	v	V	v	e	
17.	8	2	B	b	v	e	W	e	r	5	5	R	r	e	V	
18.	3	e	E	e	3	4	b	V	v	e	W	w	q	A	a	
19.	5	e	3	V	f	r	6	5	4	e	e	E	e	3	E	
20.	e	E	e	R	3	4	2	1	3	E	e	h	G	f	d	

ANSWERS TO CONCENTRATION TESTS

TEST 1

1. 3	6. 3	11. 4	16. 3
2. 4	7. 3	12. 3	17. 5
3. 3	8. 5	13. 3	18. 2
4. 3	9. 3	14. 2	19. 2
5. 2	10. 4	15. 3	20. 2

TEST 2

1. 4	6. 2	11. 4	16. 3
2. 4	7. 5	12. 1	17. 4
3. 2	8. 2	13. 3	18. 3
4. 3	9. 4	14. 2	19. 2
5. 3	10. 4	15. 1	20. 3

TEST 3

1. 4	6. 2	11. 6	16. 5
2. 4	7. 4	12. 1	17. 4
3. 4	8. 2	13. 5	18. 3
4. 4	9. 2	14. 3	19. 3
5. 2	10. 3	15. 2	20. 4

TEST 4

1. 4	6. 3	11. 4	16. 5
2. 4	7. 3	12. 3	17. 3
3. 2	8. 4	13. 4	18. 4
4. 3	9. 4	14. 4	19. 4
5. 5	10. 2	15. 2	20. 4

TEST 5

1. 5	6. 4	11. 6	16. 2
2. 3	7. 6	12. 3	17. 3
3. 2	8. 2	13. 7	18. 5
4. 2	9. 7	14. 3	19. 6
5. 6	10. 4	15. 0	20. 5

Check through your answers carefully and go back to check over the ones you got wrong.

Now move onto to the next set of five concentration tests.

CONCENTRATION TEST 1

Place a diagonal line across each box that contains 4 dots only. You have 30 seconds to complete the test.

CONCENTRATION TEST 2

Place a diagonal line across each box that contains 4 dots only. You have 30 seconds to complete the test.

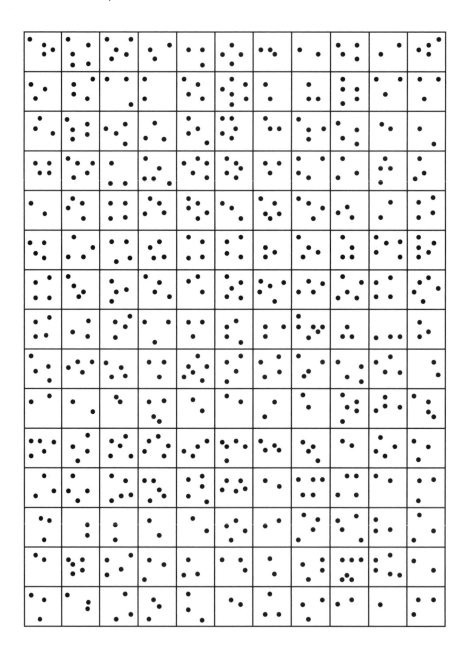

CONCENTRATION TEST 3

Place a diagonal line across each box that contains 4 dots only. You have 30 seconds to complete the test.

CONCENTRATION TEST 4

Place a diagonal line across each box that contains 4 dots only. You have 30 seconds to complete the test.

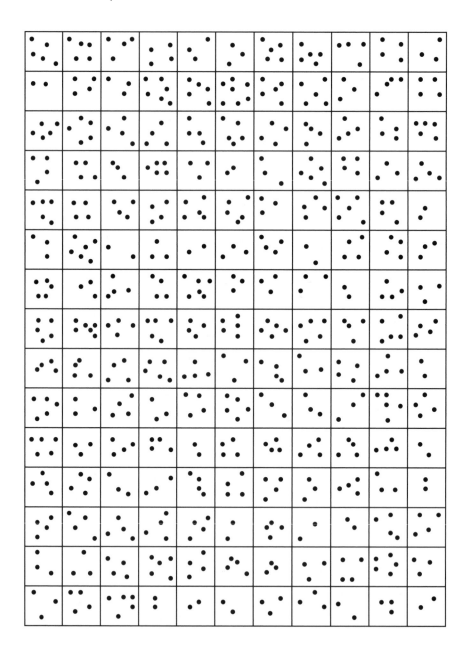

CONCENTRATION TEST 5

Place a diagonal line across each box that contains 4 dots only. You have 30 seconds to complete the test.

ANSWERS TO CONCENTRATION TESTS 1 TO 5

CONCENTRATION TEST 1

55 boxes containing groups of 4 dots

CONCENTRATION TEST 2

58 boxes containing groups of 4 dots

CONCENTRATION TEST 3

31 boxes containing groups of 4 dots

CONCENTRATION TEST 4

69 boxes containing groups of 4 dots

CONCENTRATION TEST 5

54 boxes containing groups of 4 dots

CHAPTER 5
MECHANICAL COMPREHENSION TESTS

Mechanical comprehension tests are an assessment that measures an individual's aptitude to learn mechanical skills. The tests are usually multiple choice in nature and present simple, frequently encountered mechanisms and situations. The majority of mechanical comprehension tests require a working knowledge of basic mechanical operations and the application of physical laws. On the following pages I have provided you with a number of example questions to help you prepare for the tests. Work through them as quickly as possible but remember to go back and check which ones you get wrong; more importantly, make sure you understand how the correct answer is reached.

In this particular exercise there are 20 questions and you have 10 minutes in which to answer them.

MECHANICAL COMPREHENSION TEST 1

Question 1

If Circle 'B' turns in a Clockwise direction, which way will circle 'A' turn?

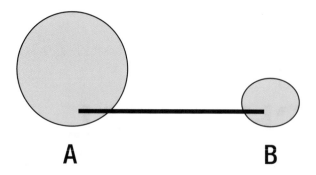

A   B

A. Clockwise

B. Anti-Clockwise

C. Backwards and forwards

D. It won't move

Answer [   ]

Question 2

Which square is carrying the heaviest load?

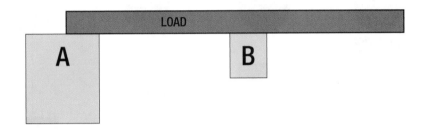

A. Square A

B. Square B

Answer [   ]

Question 3

Which pendulum will swing at the slowest speed?

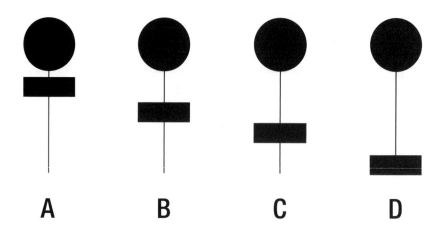

Answer [   ]

Question 4

If Cog 'A' turns in an anti-clockwise direction which way will Cog 'B' turn?

A. Clockwise

B. Anti-Clockwise

Answer

Question 5

If Cog 'B' moves in a clockwise direction, which way will Cog 'A' turn?

A. Clockwise

B. Anti-Clockwise

Answer [   ]

Question 6

Which shelf can carry the greatest load?

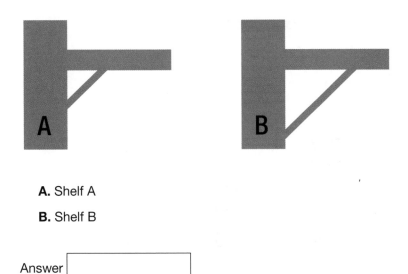

A. Shelf A

B. Shelf B

Answer [   ]

Question 7

At which point will the pendulum be travelling at the greatest speed?

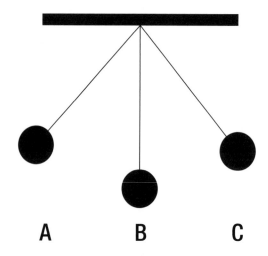

A   B   C

A. Point A

B. Point B

C. Point C

Answer _____

Question 8

At which point will the beam balance?

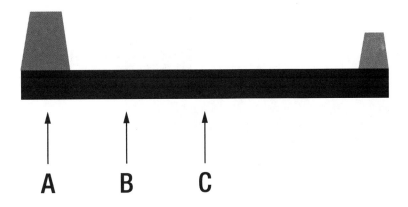

A. Point A

B. Point B

C. Point C

Answer [   ]

Question 9

If water is poured into the narrow tube, up to point 'X', what height would it reach in the wide tube?

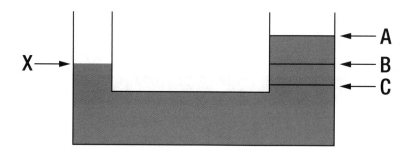

A. Point A

B. Point B

C. Point C

Answer

Question 10

At which point would Ball 'Y' have to be placed to balance out Ball 'X'?

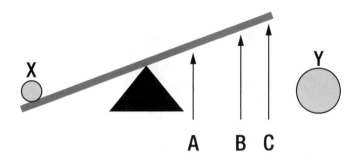

A. Point A

B. Point B

C. Point C

Answer

Question 11

If Cog 'A' turns anti-clockwise, which way will Cog 'F' turn?

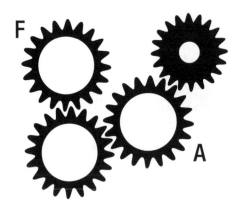

A. Cannot say

B. Clockwise

C. Anti-Clockwise

Answer

Question 12

Which post is carrying the heaviest load?

A. Both the Same

B. Post X

C. Post Y

Answer [   ]

Question 13

If water is poured in at Point D, which tube will overflow first?

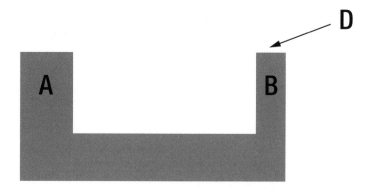

A. Tube A

B. Both the same

C. Tube B

Answer [   ]

Question 14

At which point would it be easier to haul up load X?

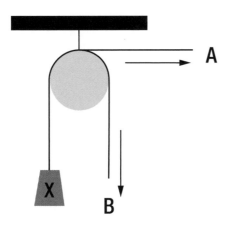

A. Both the Same

B. Point A

C. Point B

Answer [ ]

Question 15

If rope 'A' is pulled in the direction of the arrow, which way will wheel 'C' turn?

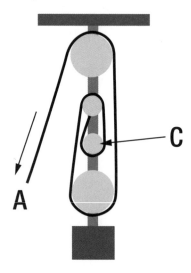

A. Clockwise

B. Anti-clockwise

C. It will not turn

Answer [   ]

Question 16

Which load is the heaviest?

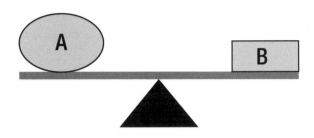

A. Both the Same

B. Load B

C. Load A

Answer _____

Question 17

If rope 'A' is pulled in the direction of the arrow, which direction will Load 'Q' travel in?

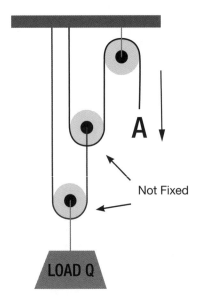

A. It will not move

B. Down

C. Up

Answer [   ]

Question 18

If circle 'X' turns anti-clockwise, which way will circle 'Y' turn?

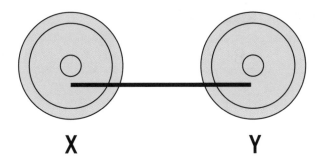

X   Y

A. Anti-clockwise

B. Clockwise

C. Backwards and forwards

Answer [   ]

Question 19

Which pulley system will be the easiest to lift the bucket of water?

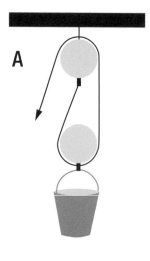
A

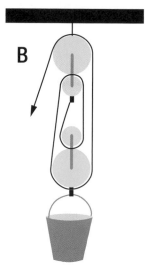
B

A. Both the Same

B. Pulley A

C. Pulley B

Answer [   ]

Question 20

At which point(s) will the pendulum be swinging the fastest?

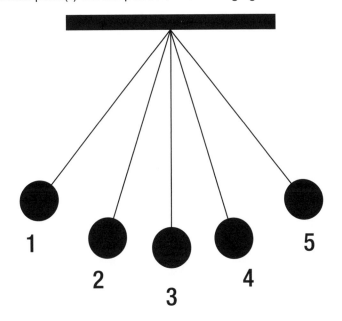

A. Point 1

B. Points 1 and 5

C. Points 3 and 5

D. Point 3

Answer

Now that you have completed mechanical comprehension exercise 1, check your answers carefully before moving onto the exercise 2.

ANSWERS TO MECHANICAL COMPREHENSION TEST 1

1.	C	**11.**	C
2.	B	**12.**	C
3.	D	**13.**	B
4.	B	**14.**	A
5.	A	**15.**	B
6.	B	**16.**	A
7.	B	**17.**	C
8.	B	**18.**	A
9.	B	**19.**	C
10.	A	**20.**	D

MECHANICAL COMPREHENSION TEST 2

During mechanical comprehension test 2 you have 10 minutes in which to answer the 20 questions.

Question 1

In the following cog and belt system, which cog will rotate the most number of times in an hour?

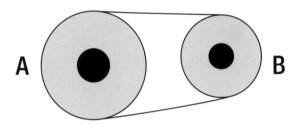

A. Cog A

B. Cog B

C. Both the same

Answer _____

Question 2

In the following cog and belt system, which cog will rotate the most number of times in thirty minutes?

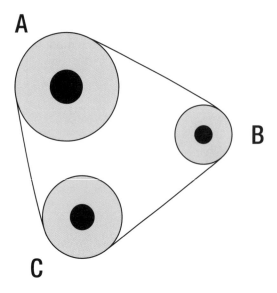

A. Cog A

B. Cog B

C. Both the same

Answer [   ]

Question 3

Which rope would be the easiest to pull the mast over with?

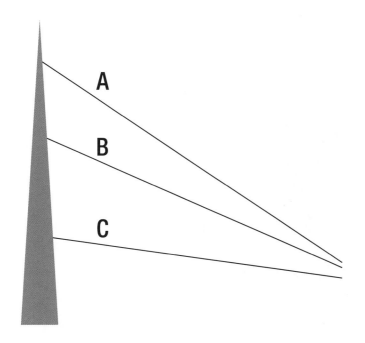

A. Rope A

B. Rope B

C. Rope C

Answer [   ]

Question 4

If cog A turns anti clockwise as indicated, which way will cog C turn?

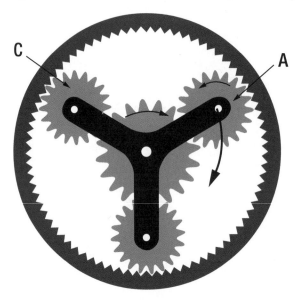

A. Clockwise

B. Anti-clockwise

C. Backwards and forwards

Answer [   ]

Question 5

If cog A turns clockwise, which way will cog D turn?

A. Clockwise

B. Anti-clockwise

C. Backwards and forwards

Answer [   ]

Question 6

If wheel D moves anticlockwise at a speed of 100 rpm, how will wheel B move and at what speed?

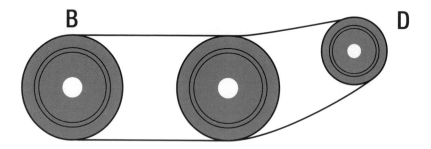

A. Clockwise faster

B. Clockwise slower

C. Anticlockwise faster

D. Anticlockwise slower

Answer _____

Question 7

Which is the best tool to use for tightening bolts?

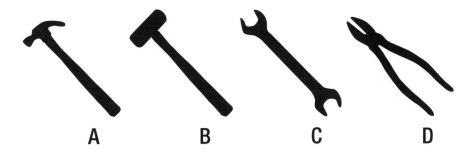

Answer ☐

Question 8

In the following circuit, if switch A closes and switch B remains open, what will happen?

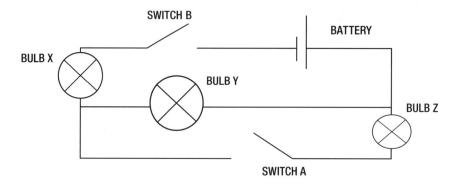

A. Bulbs X, Y, and Z will illuminate.

B. Bulb X will illuminate only.

C. Bulbs Y and Z will illuminate only.

D. No bulbs will illuminate.

Answer [　　　　　　　]

Question 9

In the following circuit, if switch A closes, what will happen?

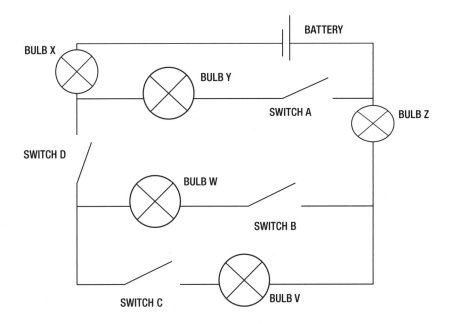

A. Bulbs V, W, X, Y, and Z will illuminate.

B. Bulb X and Y will illuminate only.

C. Bulbs X, Y and Z will illuminate only.

D. No bulbs will illuminate.

Answer _____

Question 10

The following four containers are filled with clean water to the same level, which is 2 metres in height. If you measured the pressure at the bottom of each container once filled with water, which container would register the highest reading? If you think the reading would be the same for each container then your answer should be E.

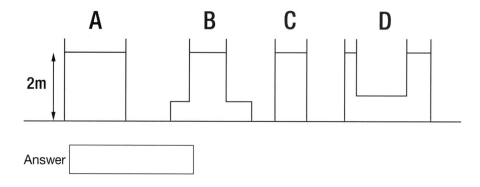

Answer [   ]

Question 11

Which of the following objects is the most unstable? If you think they're all the same then choose F for your answer.

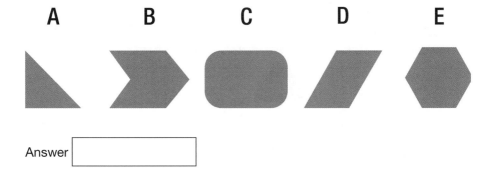

Answer [   ]

Question 12

How much weight will need to be placed at point X in order to balance out the beam?

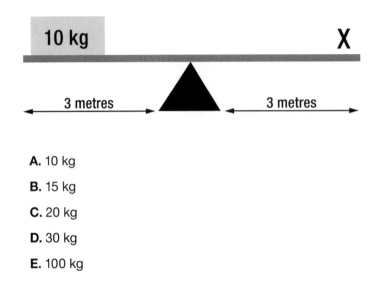

A. 10 kg

B. 15 kg

C. 20 kg

D. 30 kg

E. 100 kg

Answer [   ]

Question 13

Which post is carrying the greatest load?

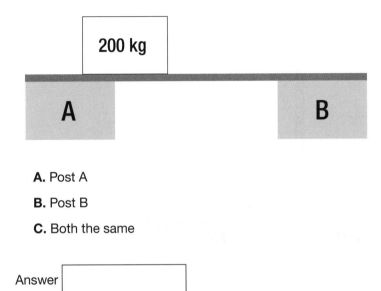

A. Post A

B. Post B

C. Both the same

Answer

Question 14

On the following weighing scales, which is the heaviest load?

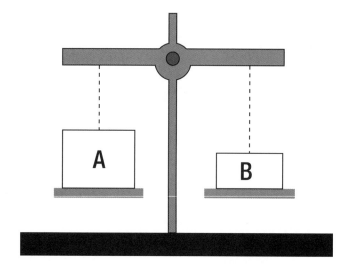

A. Load A

B. Load B

C. Both the same

Answer [   ]

Question 15

At which point should pressurised air enter the cylinder in order to force the piston downwards?

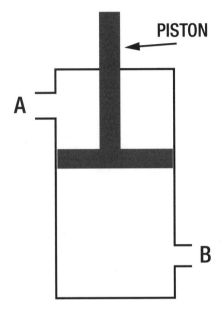

A. Point A

B. Point B

C. Both Point A and Point B

Answer _____

Question 16

At which point would you place the hook to keep the beam horizontal when lifted?

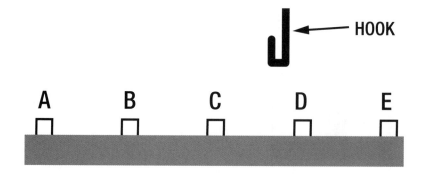

A. Point A

B. Point B

C. Point C

D. Point D

E. Point E

Answer [   ]

Question 17

At which point will the ball be travelling the fastest?

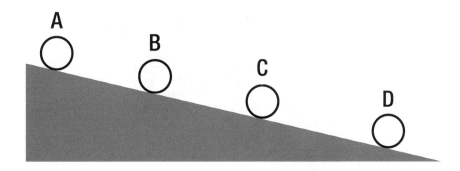

A. Point A

B. Point B

C. Point C

D. Point D

E. The same speed at each point

Answer

Question 18

If gear A moves to the right, which way will gear B move?

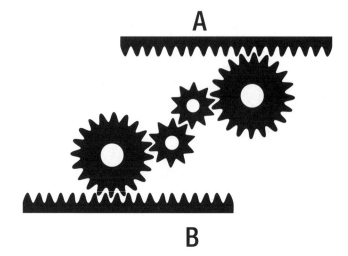

A. To the right

B. To the left

C. It won't move

D. Backwards and forward

Answer [   ]

Question 19

At which point will the beam balance?

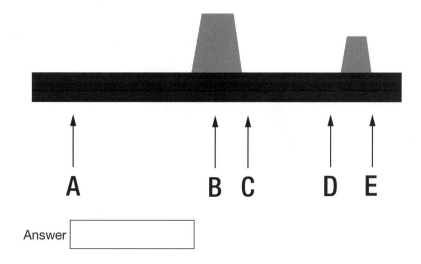

Answer [   ]

Question 20

Which is the heaviest load?

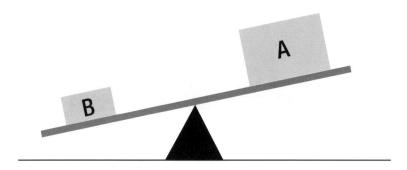

A. Load A

B. Load B

C. Both the same

Answer

Now that you have completed mechanical reasoning test 2, check your answers carefully before moving onto the next section of the guide.

ANSWERS TO MECHANICAL COMPREHENSION TEST 2

1.	B	11.	D
2.	B	12.	A
3.	A	13.	A
4.	B	14.	C
5.	B	15.	A
6.	D	16.	C
7.	C	17.	D
8.	D	18.	A
9.	B	19.	C
10.	E	20.	B

CHAPTER 6
FAULT ANALYSIS TESTS

Fault analysis tests are more commonly used during assessments for careers that require a technical level of competence. Accuracy and speed are very important during this type of test. You will normally be required to assess different dials or switches in order to identify where a particular fault lies. Alternatively, you maybe required to use 'priority checking tables' to assist you during the analysis stage, similar to the questions that now follow.

Take a look at the following 3 dials and using the 'priority for checking' table decide the order in which you would check the dials:

L   M   R

L = Left dial   M = Middle dial   R = Right dial

Priority for checking:

■ = 1st

▨ = 2nd

▢ = 3rd

Your task is to study the series of 3 dials and the arrows in each question and decide which of the multiple-choice answers is correct. In relation to the above 3 dials, and the corresponding priority checking table, the correct answer would be **LMR.** The left dial (L) must be checked first because the arrow is located through black shading, followed by the middle dial (M) and finally the right dial (R). Now work through the following sample test which has 10 questions. You have 3 minutes to complete the test. Use the 'priority for checking' table as a guide to answering the questions.

FAULT ANALYSIS TEST 1

Priority for checking:

■ = 1st

▦ = 2nd

▢ = 3rd

Question 1

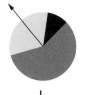

L   M   R

A. MRL

B. LRM

C. RML

D. MLR

Question 2

L   M   R

A. MRL

B. LRM

C. RML

D. MLR

Question 3

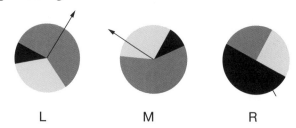

A. RML

B. RLM

C. MRL

D. MLR

Question 4

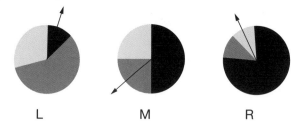

A. LMR

B. LRM

C. RML

D. MLR

Question 5

L   M   R

A. LMR

B. LRM

C. RML

D. MLR

Question 6

 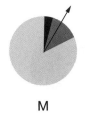

L   M   R

A. LRM

B. LMR

C. RML

D. MLR

Question 7

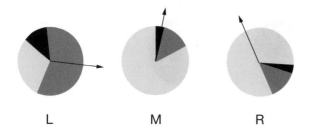

L   M   R

A. LRM

B. LMR

C. RML

D. MLR

Question 8

L   M   R

A. LRM

B. LMR

C. RML

D. MLR

Question 9

  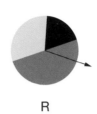

L M R

A. LRM

B. LMR

C. RML

D. MLR

Question 10

L M R

A. LRM

B. MRL

C. RML

D. MLR

ANSWERS TO FAULT ANALYSIS TEST 1

1. C
2. D
3. B
4. A
5. D
6. B
7. D
8. C
9. A
10. B

Once you have thoroughly checked through your answers, move on to sample test 2 which has 10 questions. You have 3 minutes to complete the test. Use the 'priority for checking' table as a guide to answering the questions.

FAULT ANALYSIS TEST 2

Priority for checking:

■ = 1st

■ = 2nd

□ = 3rd

Question 1

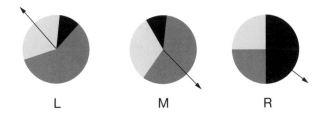

L   M   R

A. MRL

B. LRM

C. RML

D. MLR

Question 2

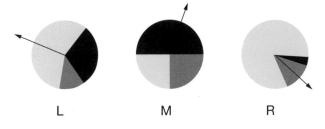

L   M   R

A. LMR

B. LRM

C. RML

D. MRL

Question 3

L   M   R

A. LMR

B. LRM

C. RML

D. MRL

Question 4

  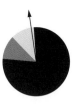

L   M   R

A. LMR

B. MLR

C. RML

D. RLM

Question 5

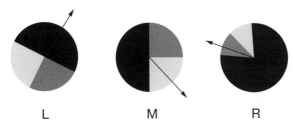

L   M   R

A. LMR

B. MLR

C. RML

D. RLM

Question 6

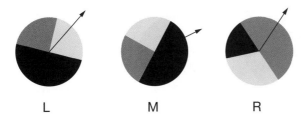

L   M   R

A. LMR

B. MLR

C. RML

D. RLM

Question 7

L   M   R

A. MRL

B. RLM

C. RML

D. LRM

Question 8

 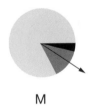

L   M   R

A. RLM

B. RML

C. LMR

D. LRM

Question 9

L	M	R

A. MRL

B. RML

C. LMR

D. LRM

Question 10

L	M	R

A. MRL

B. RML

C. LMR

D. LRM

ANSWERS TO SAMPLE TRP PART 2 TEST

1. B
2. A
3. C
4. D
5. B
6. A
7. B
8. A
9. D
10. A

FAULT ANALYSIS TEST 3

The next set of fault analysis test questions are slightly different from the 'dials' you encountered earlier.

In the following question you have to identify which of the three switches (W, Z or X) is not working. The box on the left hand side contains four circles, each labelled A, B, C and D. A key to the switches and the function they each perform is detailed below.

Which switch in the sequence is not working?

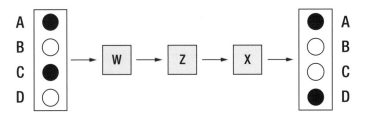

Switch	Function of the switch
W	Turns A and C on/off i.e. Black to white and vice versa
X	Turns B and D on/off i.e. Black to white and vice versa
Y	Turns C and D on/off i.e. Black to white and vice versa
Z	Turns A and D on/off i.e. Black to white and vice versa

You will notice that the box on the left contains black circles A and C, and white circles B and D at the start of the sequence. The first switch to operate is 'W', which has the effect of turning circles A and C from black to white, and vice versa. Once switch 'W' operates, the lights on the left will all be white in colour.

The next switch to operate is switch Z, which has the effect of turning circles A and D from black to white and vice versa. Because the circles contained within the box on the left hand side are all white after the operation of switch W, this now means that circles A and D are black, and circles B and C are white. You will notice that the box with the four circles located on the right hand side is now identical to this, which means that switch X must be inoperative. If it was working correctly, then the box of circles on the right hand side would look different. Therefore the correct answer to the question is switch X.

Now that you understand what is required during this test, take the time to work through the following sample Fault Analysis test. You have 5 minutes to complete the 10 questions.

FAULT ANALYSIS TEST 3

Question 1

Which switch in the sequence is not working?

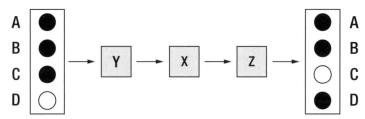

Switch	Function of the switch
W	Turns A and C on/off i.e. Black to white and vice versa
X	Turns B and D on/off i.e. Black to white and vice versa
Y	Turns C and D on/off i.e. Black to white and vice versa
Z	Turns A and D on/off i.e. Black to white and vice versa

Answer

Question 2

Which switch in the sequence is not working?

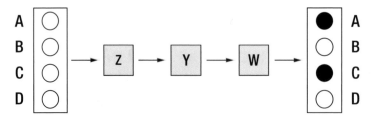

Switch	Function of the switch
W	Turns A and C on/off i.e. Black to white and vice versa
X	Turns B and D on/off i.e. Black to white and vice versa
Y	Turns C and D on/off i.e. Black to white and vice versa
Z	Turns A and D on/off i.e. Black to white and vice versa

Answer [   ]

Question 3

Which switch in the sequence is not working?

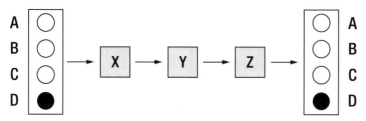

Switch	Function of the switch
W	Turns A and C on/off i.e. Black to white and vice versa
X	Turns B and D on/off i.e. Black to white and vice versa
Y	Turns C and D on/off i.e. Black to white and vice versa
Z	Turns A and D on/off i.e. Black to white and vice versa

Answer

Question 4

Which switch in the sequence is not working?

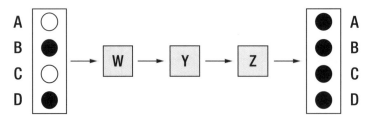

Switch	Function of the switch
W	Turns A and C on/off i.e. Black to white and vice versa
X	Turns B and D on/off i.e. Black to white and vice versa
Y	Turns C and D on/off i.e. Black to white and vice versa
Z	Turns A and D on/off i.e. Black to white and vice versa

Answer [   ]

Question 5

Which switch in the sequence is not working?

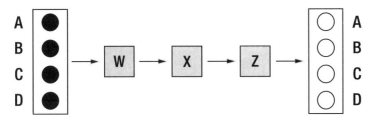

Switch	Function of the switch
W	Turns A and C on/off i.e. Black to white and vice versa
X	Turns B and D on/off i.e. Black to white and vice versa
Y	Turns C and D on/off i.e. Black to white and vice versa
Z	Turns A and D on/off i.e. Black to white and vice versa

Answer [   ]

Question 6

Which switch in the sequence is not working?

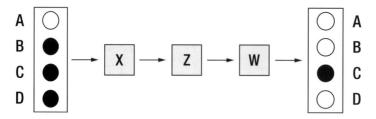

Switch	Function of the switch
W	Turns A and C on/off i.e. Black to white and vice versa
X	Turns B and D on/off i.e. Black to white and vice versa
Y	Turns C and D on/off i.e. Black to white and vice versa
Z	Turns A and D on/off i.e. Black to white and vice versa

Answer [   ]

Question 7

Which switch in the sequence is not working?

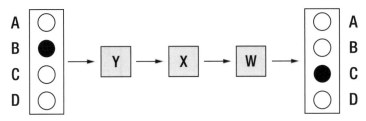

Switch	Function of the switch
W	Turns A and C on/off i.e. Black to white and vice versa
X	Turns B and D on/off i.e. Black to white and vice versa
Y	Turns C and D on/off i.e. Black to white and vice versa
Z	Turns A and D on/off i.e. Black to white and vice versa

Answer

Question 8

Which switch in the sequence is not working?

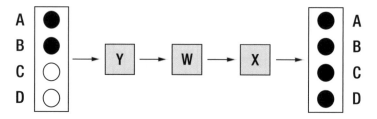

Switch	Function of the switch
W	Turns A and C on/off i.e. Black to white and vice versa
X	Turns B and D on/off i.e. Black to white and vice versa
Y	Turns C and D on/off i.e. Black to white and vice versa
Z	Turns A and D on/off i.e. Black to white and vice versa

Answer [ ]

Question 9

Which switch in the sequence is not working?

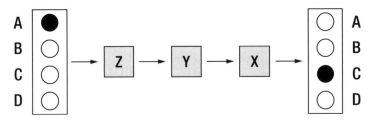

Switch	Function of the switch
W	Turns A and C on/off i.e. Black to white and vice versa
X	Turns B and D on/off i.e. Black to white and vice versa
Y	Turns C and D on/off i.e. Black to white and vice versa
Z	Turns A and D on/off i.e. Black to white and vice versa

Answer [   ]

Question 10

Which switch in the sequence is not working?

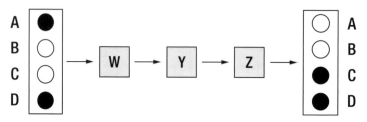

Switch	Function of the switch
W	Turns A and C on/off i.e. Black to white and vice versa
X	Turns B and D on/off i.e. Black to white and vice versa
Y	Turns C and D on/off i.e. Black to white and vice versa
Z	Turns A and D on/off i.e. Black to white and vice versa

Answer _____

ANSWERS TO FAULT ANALYSIS TEST

1.   Switch X
2.   Switch W
3.   Switch X
4.   Switch Y
5.   Switch Z
6.   Switch Z
7.   Switch W
8.   Switch W
9.   Switch X
10. Switch Y

USEFUL LINKS AND RESOURCES

During this section of the guide I have provided you with some useful links and resources, many of which are free to use.

Free online psychometric tests	psychometrictestsonline.co.uk
Speed, distance and time test questions	speeddistancetime.info
Numerical tests	kent.ac.uk/careers/tests/mathstest.htm
Verbal reasoning tests	kent.ac.uk/careers/tests/verbaltest.htm
Logical reasoning tests	kent.ac.uk/careers/tests/sequences.htm
SHL – provider of behavioural and ability assessment tools	shl.com

A FEW FINAL WORDS

You have now reached the end of the guide and no doubt you will want to try further psychometric test questions. We have provided you with FREE online psychometric test questions at the following website:

psychometrictestsonline.co.uk

Just before you go off and practice some more questions, consider the following. The majority of candidates who pass their psychometric tests have a number of common factors. These are as follows:

1. *They believe in themselves.*

The first factor is self-belief. Regardless of what anyone tells you, you can pass your psychometric test assessment and achieve high scores in the process. Make sure you have the self-belief to pass the tests and fill your mind with positive thoughts.

2. *They prepare fully.*

The second factor is preparation. Those people who achieve in life prepare fully for every eventuality and that is what you must do when you are preparing for your psychometric tests. Work very hard and especially concentrate on your weaker testing areas.

Good luck in your tests.

Work hard, stay focused and be what you want…

Richard McMunn

Richard McMunn

Visit www.how2become.co.uk to find more titles and courses that will help you to pass your psychometric tests or assessment centre:

- Psychometric tests CD ROM.
- 1 Day intensive training courses.
- Psychometric testing books and online tests.

how2become.co.uk